Table of Contents

Consonants Review 2	Long Vowel Practice: *o* 92
Short and Long Vowels 24	Long Vowel Practice: *u* 100
Short Vowels 25	*Y* as Long *i* and Long *e* Sounds 108
Short Vowel Practice: *a* 26	Long and Short Vowel Review 110
Short Vowel Practice: *e* 34	Rhyming Words 112
Short Vowel Practice: *i* 42	Beginning Letter Sounds 113
Short Vowel Practice: *o* 50	Ending Letter Sounds 124
Short Vowel Practice: *u* 58	Beginning and Ending Sounds 133
Rhyming Words 66	Consonant Blends 138
Long Vowels 67	Consonant Blends with *s* 139
Long Vowel Practice: *a* 68	Consonant Blends with *r* 146
Long Vowel Practice: *e* 76	Consonant Blends with *l* 153
Long Vowel Practice: *i* 84	Certificate 160

Grades K-1 Phonics Advantage © Chalkboard Publishing Inc.

Consonants Review

Consonant Review: B

Say the name of the object. These words begin with letter sound **b**. Print the letter **b** at the beginning of each word.

 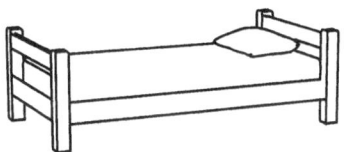 

Color the ball.	blue	Color the bus.	yellow
Color the bat.	black	Color the bed.	red
Color the boat.	brown	Color the book.	green

Consonant Review: C

Say the name of the object. These words begin with letter sound *c*. Print the letter *c* at the beginning of each word.

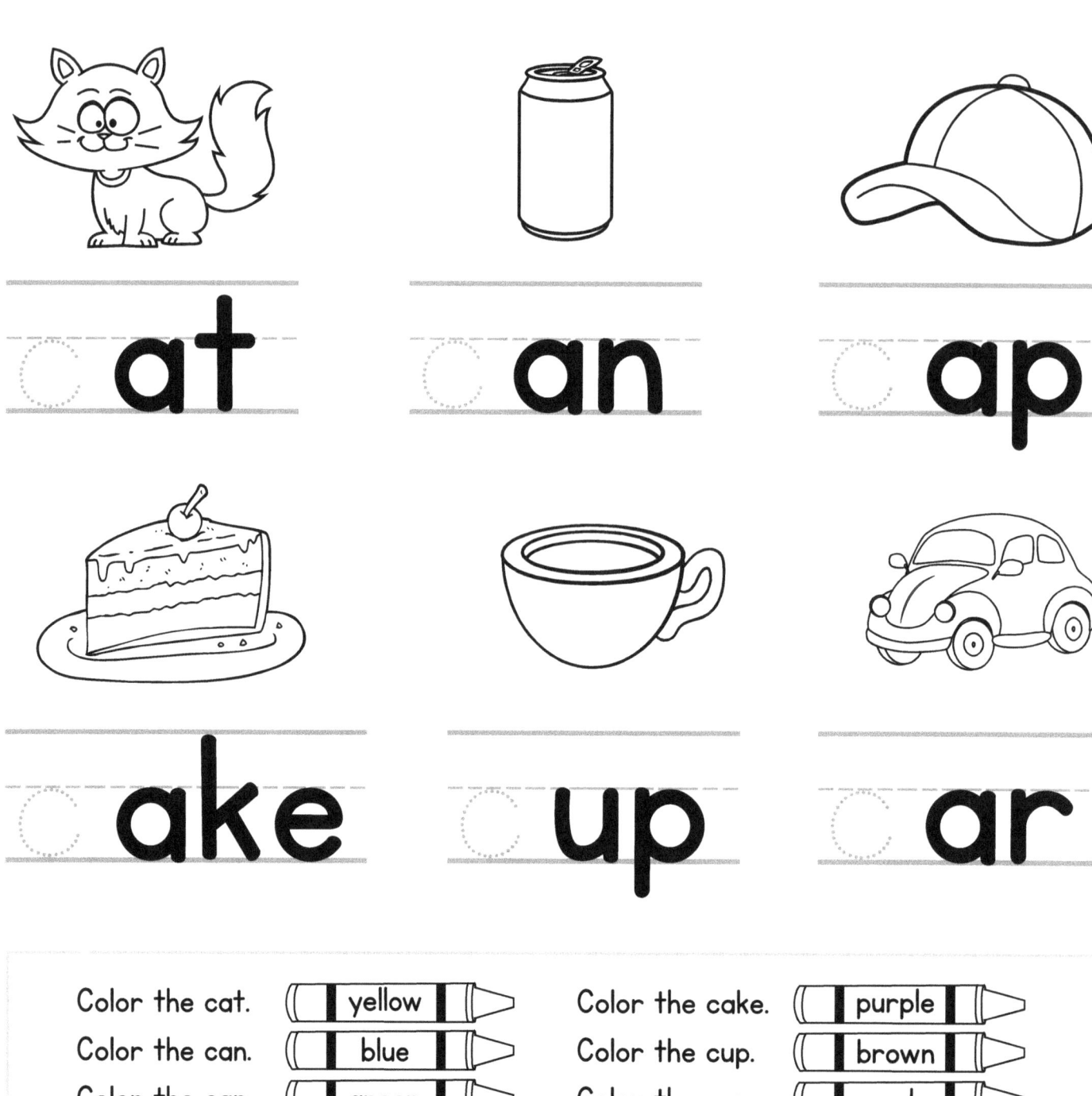

Consonant Review: D

Say the name of the object. These words begin with letter sound **d**. Print the letter **d** at the beginning of each word.

 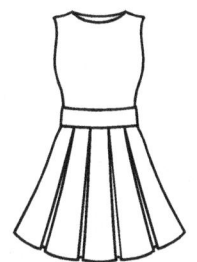 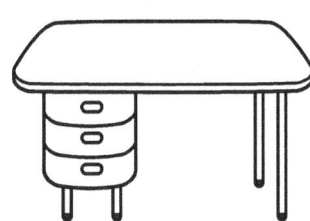

og ress esk

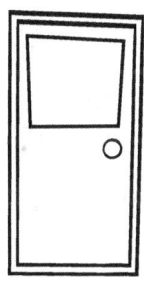  

oor uck oll

Color the dog. black   Color the door. brown
Color the dress. yellow   Color the duck. orange
Color the desk. blue   Color the doll. green

© Chalkboard Publishing Inc.

5

Consonant Review: F

Say the name of the object. These words begin with letter sound *f*. Print the letter *f* at the beginning of each word.

an   ence   ish

ork   oot   rog

Color the fan.	black	Color the fork.	brown
Color the fence.	yellow	Color the foot.	orange
Color the fish.	blue	Color the frog.	green

Consonant Review: G

Say the name of the object. These words begin with letter sound *g*. Print the letter *g* at the beginning of each word.

  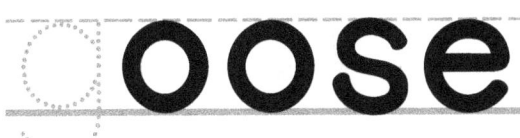

girl goat goose

 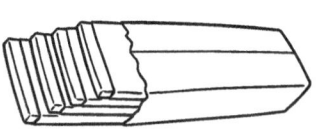 

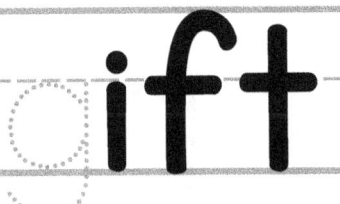 gum guitar

gift

Color the girl.	green	Color the gift.	red
Color the goat.	blue	Color the gum.	orange
Color the goose.	yellow	Color the guitar.	brown

© Chalkboard Publishing Inc.

Consonant Review: H

Say the name of the object. These words begin with letter sound **h**. Print the letter **h** at the beginning of each word.

_at   _and   _ouse

_en   _eart   _ippo

Color the hat. — black   Color the hen. — brown
Color the hand. — yellow   Color the heart. — red
Color the house. — blue   Color the hippo. — green

Consonant Review: J

Say the name of the object. These words begin with letter sound *j*. Print the letter *j* at the beginning of each word.

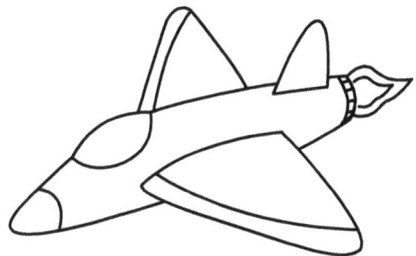

ar   et   eep

ug   elly   am

Color the jar.  blue	Color the jug.  brown
Color the jet. red	Color the jelly. orange
Color the jeep.  green	Color the jam.  purple

© Chalkboard Publishing Inc.

Consonant Review: K

Say the name of the object. These words begin with letter sound **k**. Print the letter **k** at the beginning of each word.

kite

kitten

key

king

kettle

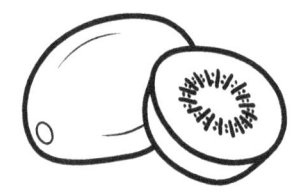
kiwi

Color the kite.   black
Color the kitten. yellow
Color the key.   blue
Color the king.   brown
Color the kettle. orange
Color the kiwi.   green

Consonant Review: L

Say the name of the object. These words begin with letter sound *l*. Print the letter *l* at the beginning of each word.

___ion   ___ock   ___amb

___og   ___eaf   ___amp

Color the lion.	red	Color the log.	brown
Color the lock.	black	Color the leaf.	green
Color the lamb.	purple	Color the lamp.	blue

Consonant Review: M

Say the name of the object. These words begin with letter sound **m**. Print the letter **m** at the beginning of each word.

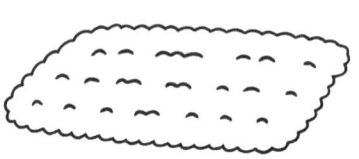

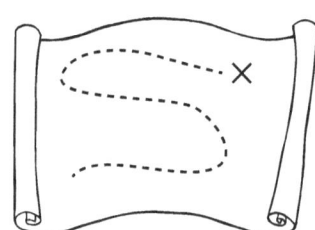

mat   moon   map

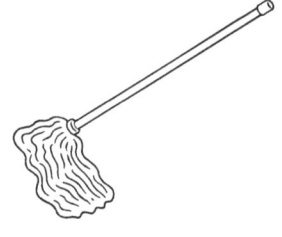

mop   milk   mouse

Color the mat.   yellow   Color the mop.   brown
Color the moon. blue   Color the milk.   orange
Color the map.   red   Color the mouse. green

Consonant Review: N

Say the name of the object. These words begin with letter sound **n**. Print the letter **n** at the beginning of each word.

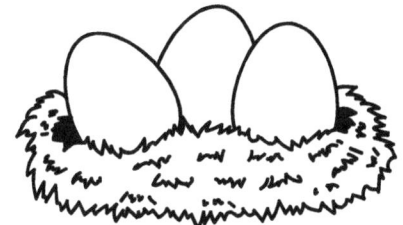

net nest nut

nail nose note

Color the net.	black	Color the nail.	blue
Color the nest.	yellow	Color the nose.	red
Color the nut.	brown	Color the note.	green

© Chalkboard Publishing Inc.

Consonant Review: P

Say the name of the object. These words begin with letter sound *p*. Print the letter *p* at the beginning of each word.

 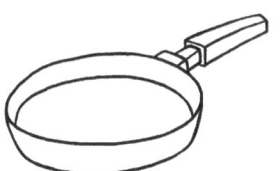 

  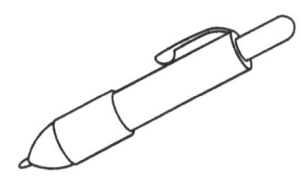

Color the paw. — black
Color the pan. — blue
Color the pie. — red
Color the pail. — purple
Color the pig. — orange
Color the pen. — green

Consonant Review: Q

Say the name of the object. These words begin with letter sound **q**. Print the letter **q** at the beginning of each word.

queen   quail   quilt

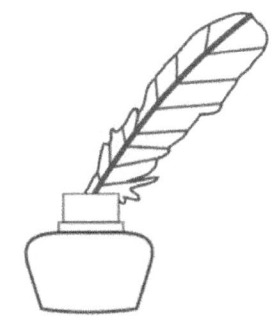 

 question

Color the queen.	yellow	Color the quill.	brown
Color the quail.	red	Color the	
Color the quilt.	blue	question mark.	orange

Consonant Review: R

Say the name of the object. These words begin with letter sound **r**.
Print the letter **r** at the beginning of each word.

  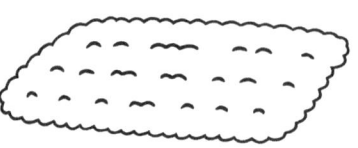

Color the rat. black   Color the rake. brown
Color the rain. yellow   Color the ring. orange
Color the rug. blue   Color the rose. green

Consonant Review: S

Say the name of the object. These words begin with letter sound **s**. Print the letter **s** at the beginning of each word.

 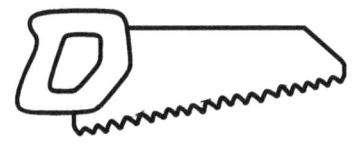 

sun **saw** **spoon**

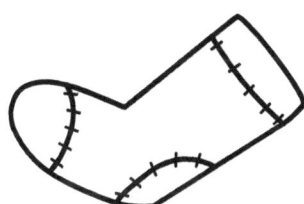  

sock **snake** **soap**

Color the sun.	orange	Color the sock.	brown
Color the saw.	blue	Color the snake.	red
Color the spoon.	green	Color the soap.	yellow

© Chalkboard Publishing Inc.

Consonant Review: T

Say the name of the object. These words begin with letter sound *t*. Print the letter *t* at the beginning of each word.

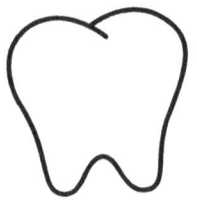 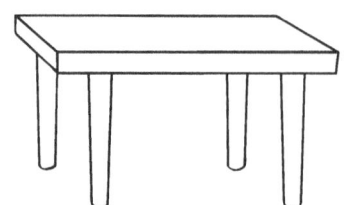 

_ooth   _able   _ub

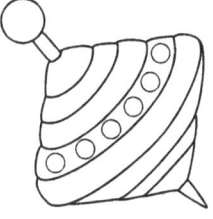  

_op   _rain   _ree

Color the tooth.	blue	Color the top.	orange
Color the table.	yellow	Color the train.	purple
Color the tub.	red	Color the tree.	green

© Chalkboard Publishing Inc.

Consonant Review: V

Say the name of the object. These words begin with letter sound **v**. Print the letter **v** at the beginning of each word.

vase　　vest　　violin

vulture　　van　　vine

Color the vase.	red	Color the vulture.	brown
Color the vest.	yellow	Color the van.	black
Color the violin.	blue	Color the vine.	green

Consonant Review: W

Say the name of the object. These words begin with letter sound **w**. Print the letter **w** at the beginning of each word.

  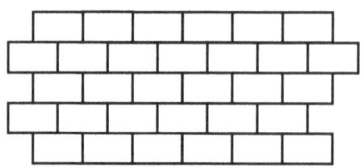

web   walrus   wall

well   worm   wagon

Color the web.	black	Color the well.	green
Color the walrus.	blue	Color the worm.	yellow
Color the wall.	red	Color the wagon.	purple

20 © Chalkboard Publishing Inc.

Consonant Review: X

Say the name of the object. These words begin with letter sound **x**.
Print the letter **x** at the beginning of each word.

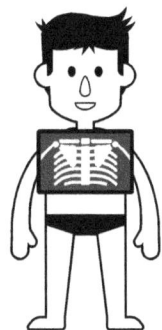
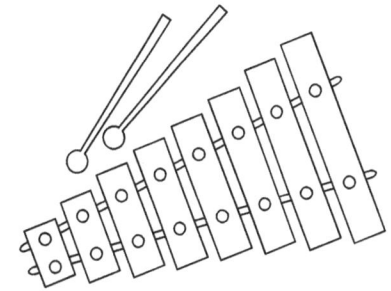

X-ray   xylophone

X-ray fish

Color the X-ray.   ⬚ black   Color the X-ray fish.   ⬚ yellow
Color the xylophone.   ⬚ blue

Consonant Review: Y

Say the name of the object. These words begin with letter sound **y**. Print the letter **y** at the beginning of each word.

yarn   yam   yoyo

yolk   yak   yeti

Color the yarn.	orange	Color the yolk.	yellow
Color the yam.	red	Color the yak.	brown
Color the yoyo.	blue	Color the yeti.	green

Consonant Review: Z

Say the name of the object. These words begin with letter sound *z*. Print the letter *z* at the beginning of each word.

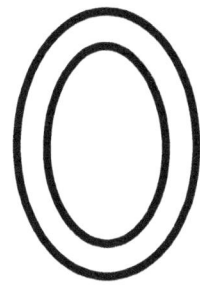  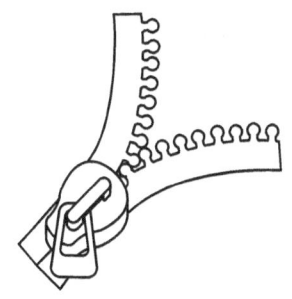

 ero zoo zipper

zebra zucchini

Color the zero.   black   Color the zebra.   brown
Color the zoo.   yellow   Color the zucchini.   green
Color the zipper.   blue

Short and Long Vowels

Long vowels say their name. Short vowels make different sounds. Read the examples below, say the names of the objects out loud.

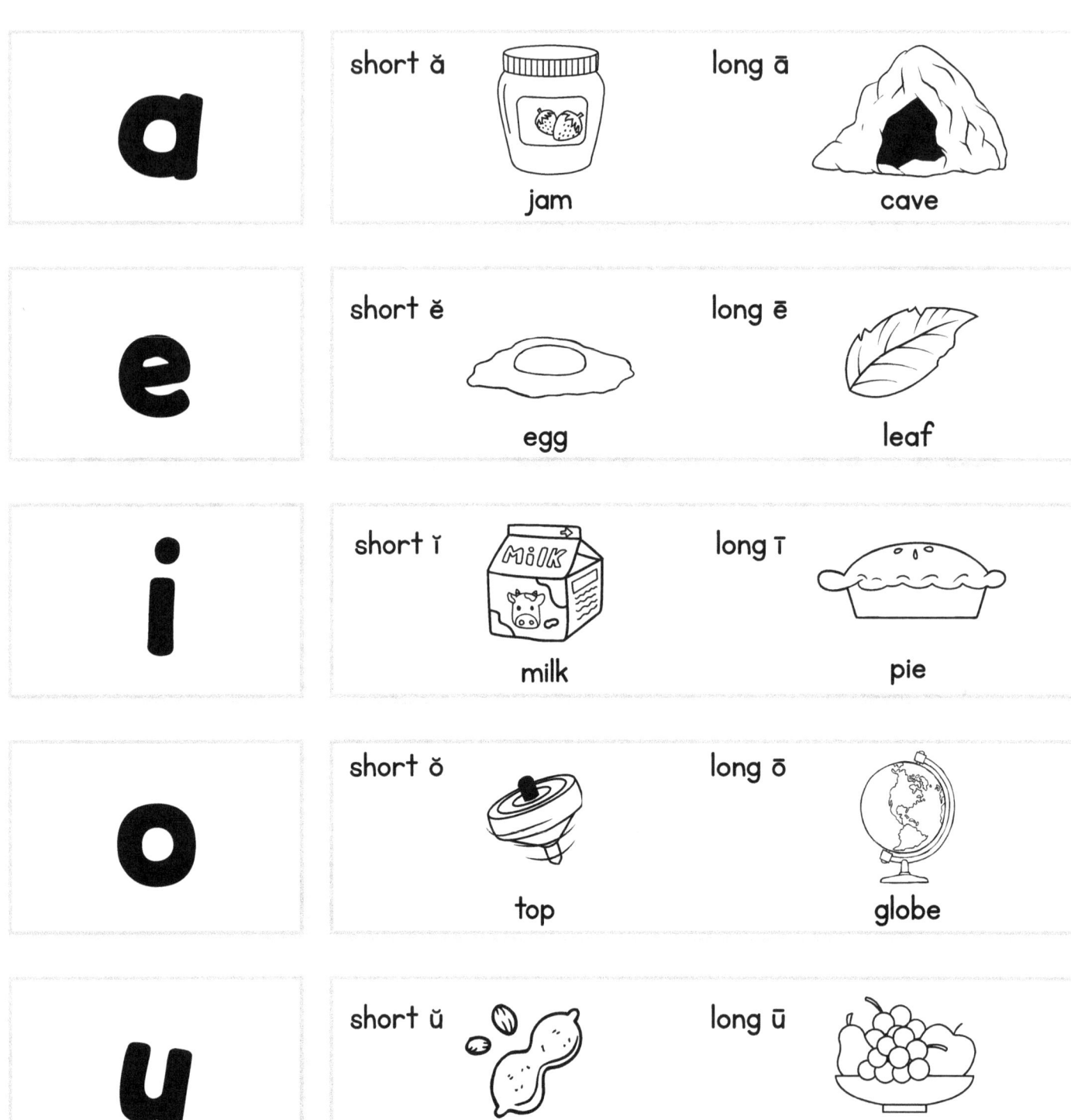

Short Vowels

Short Vowel Practice: a

Say the name of the object out loud. Listen for the short ă sound. Use the color key to color the pictures.

fan

cat

map
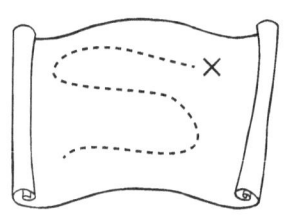

cap

jam

bag
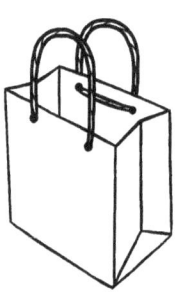

Color the fan.   purple   Color the cap.   blue
Color the cat.   brown   Color the jam.   red
Color the map.   yellow   Color the bag.   green

Short Vowel Practice: a

Say the name of the object out loud. Listen for the short ă sound. Use the color key to color the pictures.

pan
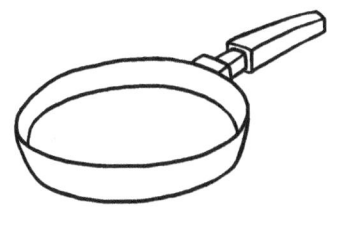

cab

rat

bat

hat

can
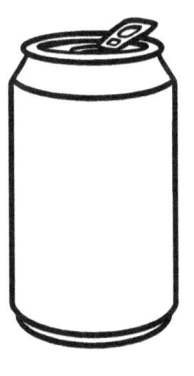

Color the pan. 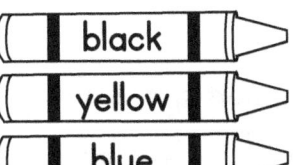 black
Color the cab. yellow
Color the rat. blue

Color the bat. 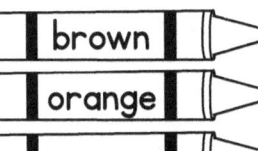 brown
Color the hat. orange
Color the can. green

© Chalkboard Publishing Inc.

Short Vowel Practice: a

Say the name of the object out loud. Fill in the missing vowel for each word. Use the color key to color the pictures.

h _ t   m _ p   c _ b

b _ g   c _ t   j _ m

Color the hat. — purple
Color the map. — brown
Color the cab. — yellow
Color the bag. — blue
Color the cat. — red
Color the jam. — green

Short Vowel Practice: a

Say the name of the object out loud. Fill in the missing vowel for each word. Use the color key to color the pictures.

p _ n   c _ p   f _ n

b _ t   c _ n   r _ t

Color the pan.	green	Color the bat.	brown
Color the cap.	yellow	Color the fan.	orange
Color the rat.	blue	Color the can.	black

Short Vowel Practice: a

Say the name of the object out loud.
Draw a line from the object to the matching word.

jam

hat

bag

bat

map

cat

Short Vowel Practice: a

Say the name of the object out loud.
Draw a line from the object to the matching word.

can

rat

cab

pan

cap

fan

Short Vowel Practice: a

Say the name of the object out loud.
Find the word. Look across for the word. Circle the word.

bag   bat   cat   hat   jam   rat

b a g c l w e
v d k c a t r
r a t f o q d
s c n e j a m
h a t r w b p
k c n b a t q

Short Vowel Practice: a

Say the name of the object out loud.
Find the word. Look across for the word. Circle the word.

cab   can   cap   fan   map   pan

z	c	a	n	l	s	d
u	o	f	p	a	n	j
c	a	b	l	e	w	g
k	r	p	b	f	a	n
e	c	a	p	w	s	z
m	a	p	i	v	p	s

© Chalkboard Publishing Inc.

Short Vowel Practice: e

Say the name of the object out loud. Listen for the short ĕ sound. Use the color key to color the pictures.

gem

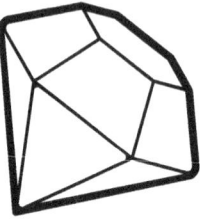

leg

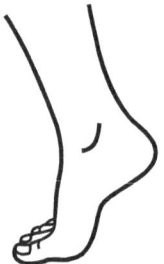

hen

bed

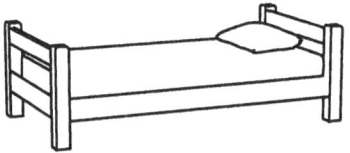

egg

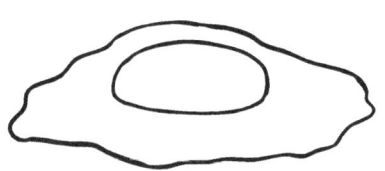

jet

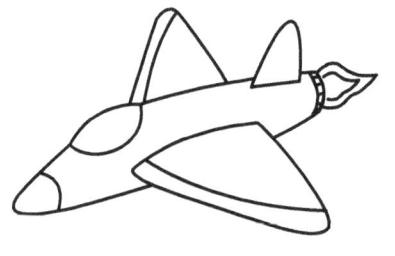

Color the gem. — blue
Color the leg. — red
Color the hen. — yellow

Color the bed. — orange
Color the egg. — green
Color the jet. — black

Short Vowel Practice: e

Say the name of the object out loud. Listen for the short ĕ sound. Use the color key to color the pictures.

well

nest
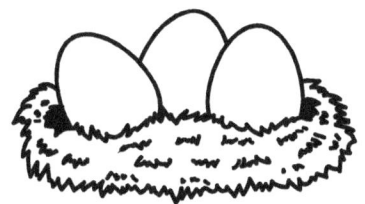

pen

ten
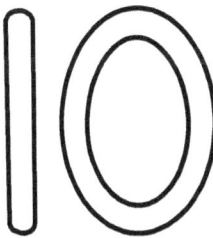

vest
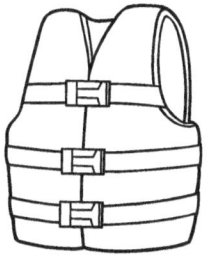

net

Color the well. — black
Color the nest. — brown
Color the pen. — purple

Color the ten. — green
Color the vest. — red
Color the net. — orange

Short Vowel Practice: e

Say the name of the object out loud. Fill in the missing vowel for each word. Use the color key to color the pictures.

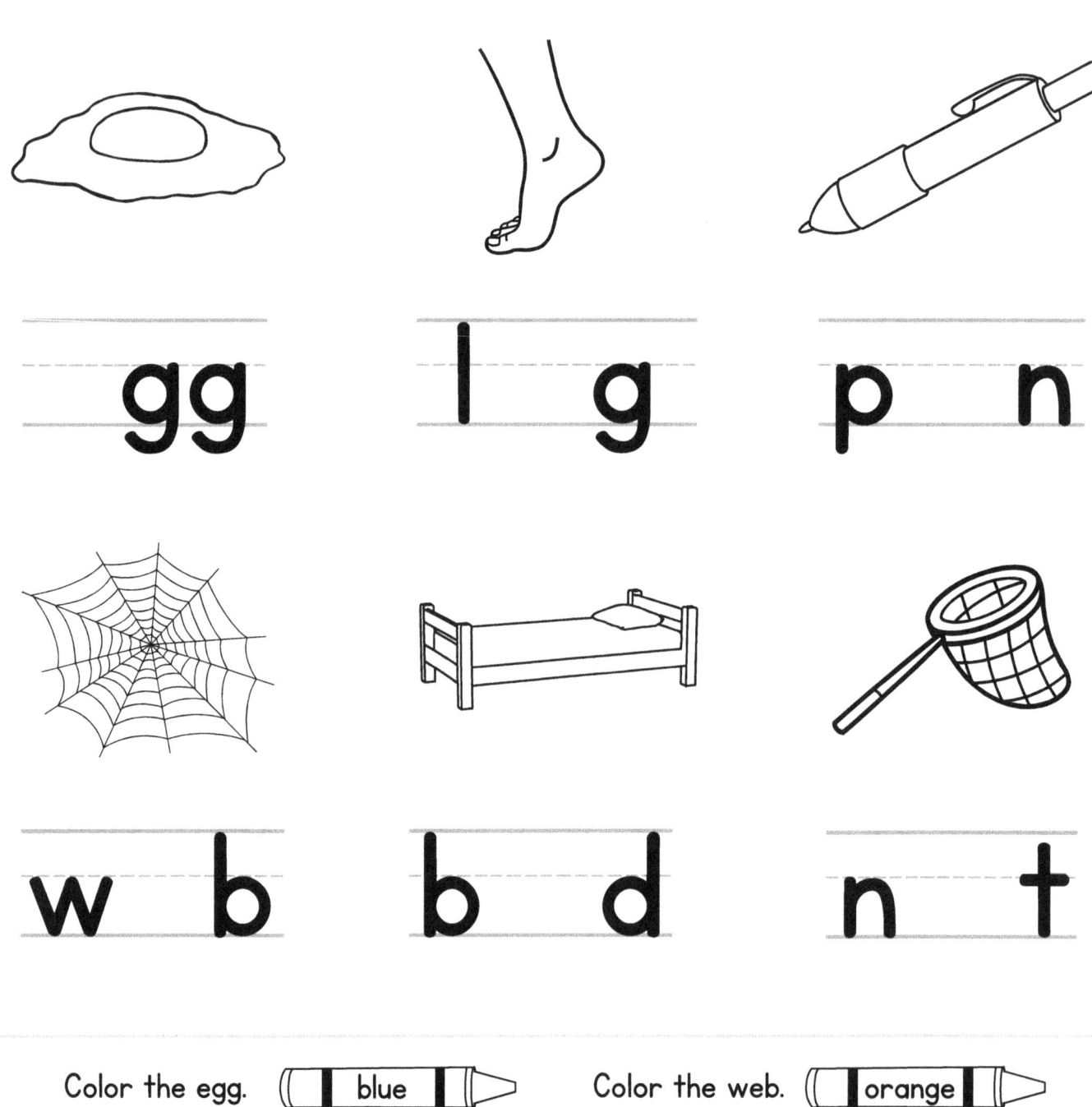

Color the egg. — blue
Color the leg. — red
Color the pen. — yellow
Color the web. — orange
Color the bed. — green
Color the net. — black

Short Vowel Practice: e

Say the name of the object out loud. Fill in the missing vowel for each word. Use the color key to color the pictures.

j_t   t_n   v_st

w_ll   h_n   g_m

Color the jet.	black	Color the well.	green
Color the ten.	brown	Color the hen.	red
Color the vest.	purple	Color the gem.	orange

Short Vowel Practice: e

Say the name of the object out loud.
Draw a line from the object to the matching word.

   leg

   bed

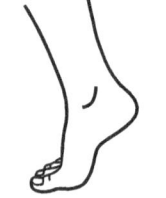   pen

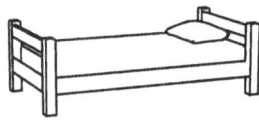   egg

   net

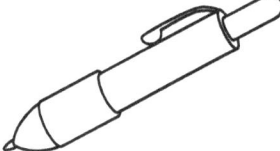   web

Short Vowel Practice: e

Say the name of the object out loud.
Draw a line from the object to the matching word.

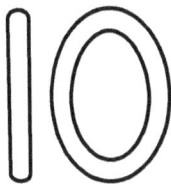 jet

 vest

 well

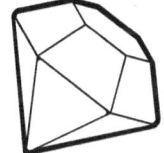 ten

 gem

 hen

Short Vowel Practice: e

Say the name of the object out loud.
Find the word. Look across for the word. Circle the word.

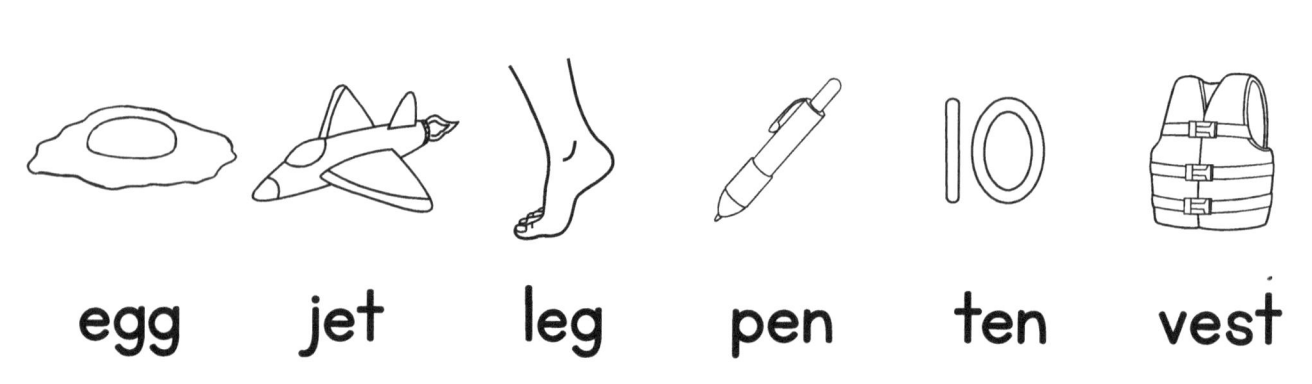

egg   jet   leg   pen   ten   vest

b a e g g w e
v d p e n t r
r j e t o q d
s c n l e g t
f t e n w b p
k c n v e s t

Short Vowel Practice: e

Say the name of the object out loud.
Find the word. Look across for the word. Circle the word.

bed   gem   hen   net   web   well

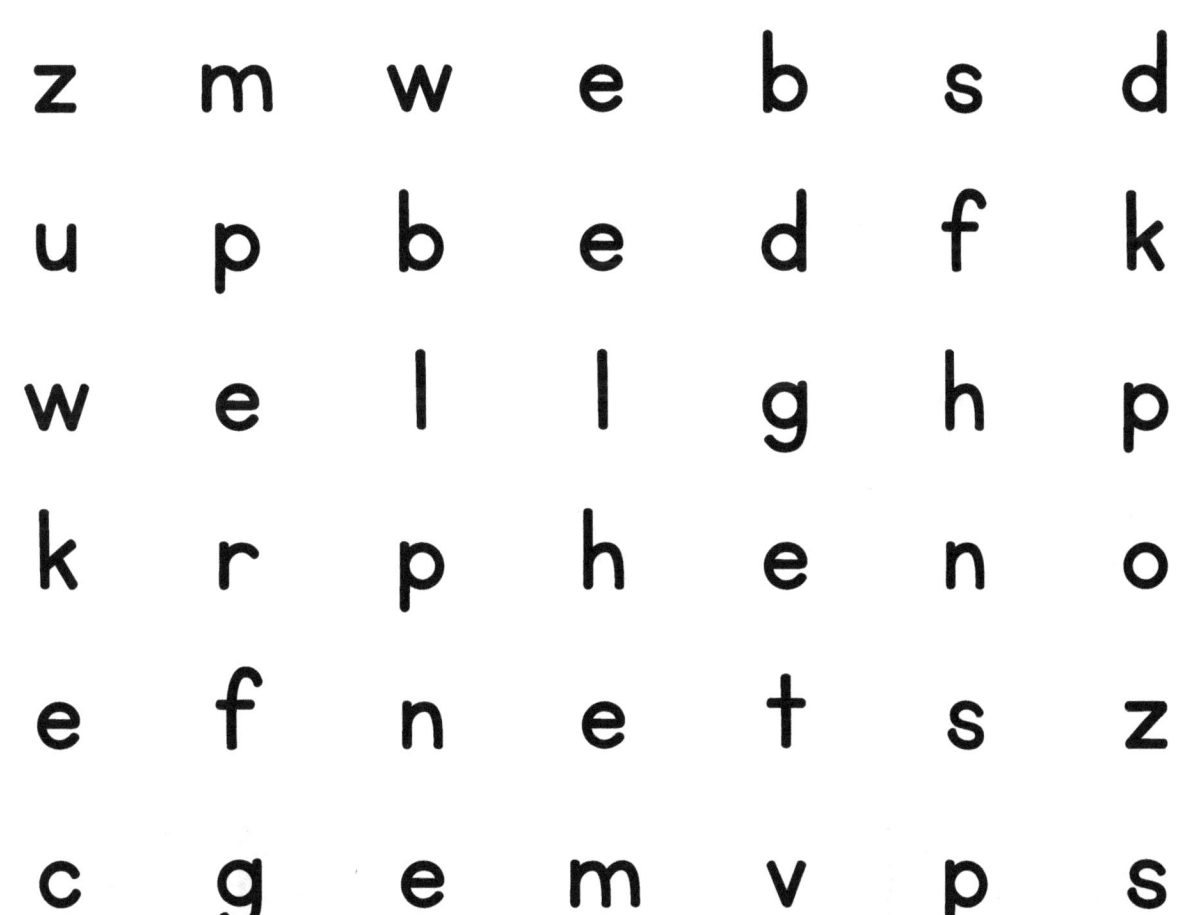

Short Vowel Practice: i

Say the name of the object out loud. Listen for the short *i* sound. Use the color key to color the pictures.

six

mitten

king

milk

igloo

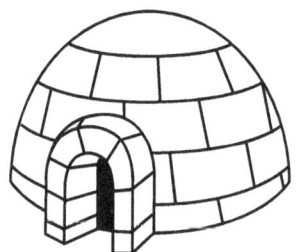

pin

Color the six.	red	Color the milk.	blue
Color the mitten.	brown	Color the igloo.	purple
Color the king.	yellow	Color the pin.	green

Short Vowel Practice: i

Say the name of the object out loud. Listen for the short *i* sound. Use the color key to color the pictures.

kid

kitten

fish

fin

gift

pig

Color the kid. purple
Color the kitten. red
Color the fish. blue

Color the fin. green
Color the gift. orange
Color the pig. pink

Short Vowel Practice: i

Say the name of the object out loud. Fill in the missing vowel for each word. Use the color key to color the pictures.

s __ x   m __ tten   k __ ng

 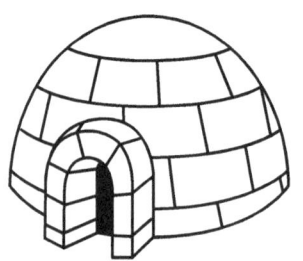 

m __ lk   __ gloo   p __ n

Color the six.	red	Color the milk.	blue
Color the mitten.	brown	Color the igloo.	purple
Color the king.	yellow	Color the pin.	green

Short Vowel Practice: i

Say the name of the object out loud. Fill in the missing vowel for each word. Use the color key to color the pictures.

k_d   k_tten   f_sh

f_n   g_ft   p_g

Color the kid. — purple
Color the kitten. — red
Color the fish. — blue
Color the fin. — green
Color the gift. — orange
Color the pig. — yellow

Short Vowel Practice: i

Say the name of the object out loud.
Draw a line from the object to the matching word.

   kid

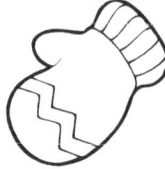   milk

   mitten

   king

   fish

   six

Short Vowel Practice: i

Say the name of the object out loud.
Draw a line from the object to the matching word.

fin

gift

kitten

pig

igloo

pin

Short Vowel Practice: i

Say the name of the object out loud.
Find the word. Look across for the word. Circle the word.

fin   igloo   king   mitten   pin   six

u	k	l	p	i	n	w
i	g	l	o	o	h	r
a	p	k	i	n	g	d
s	f	i	n	q	w	h
m	i	t	t	e	n	p
k	c	n	b	s	i	x

Short Vowel Practice: i

Say the name of the object out loud.
Find the word. Look across for the word. Circle the word.

fish   gift   kid   kitten   milk   pig

```
k  i  d  l  a  v  d
u  j  i  p  i  g  k
g  i  f  t  e  w  g
j  r  f  i  s  h  c
z  k  i  t  t  e  n
t  m  i  l  k  l  s
```

Short Vowel Practice: o

Say the name of the object out loud. Listen for the short ŏ sound. Use the color key to color the pictures.

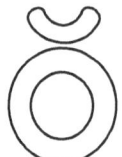

log

top
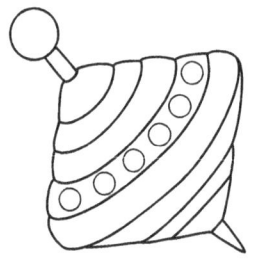

hog

doll

mop
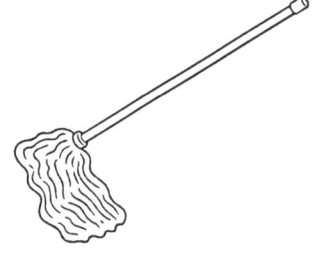

box

Color the log.	brown	Color the doll.	yellow
Color the top.	red	Color the mop.	purple
Color the hog.	blue	Color the box.	green

Short Vowel Practice: o

Say the name of the object out loud. Listen for the short ŏ sound. Use the color key to color the pictures.

sock

fox

frog

pot

dog

rod
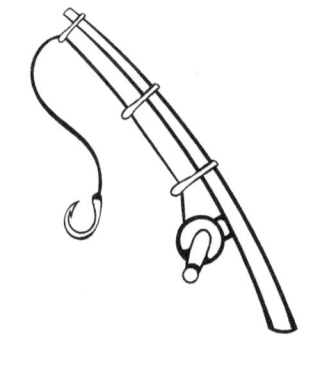

Color the sock. 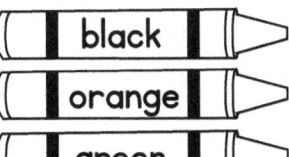 black
Color the fox. orange
Color the frog. green

Color the pot. 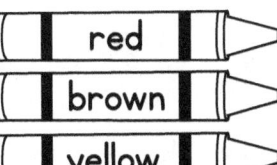 red
Color the dog. brown
Color the rod. yellow

Short Vowel Practice: o

Say the name of the object out loud. Fill in the missing vowel for each word. Use the color key to color the pictures.

l_g   t_p   h_g

d_ll   m_p   b_x

Color the log. brown
Color the top. red
Color the hog. blue
Color the doll. orange
Color the mop. purple
Color the box. green

Short Vowel Practice: o

Say the name of the object out loud. Fill in the missing vowel for each word. Use the color key to color the pictures.

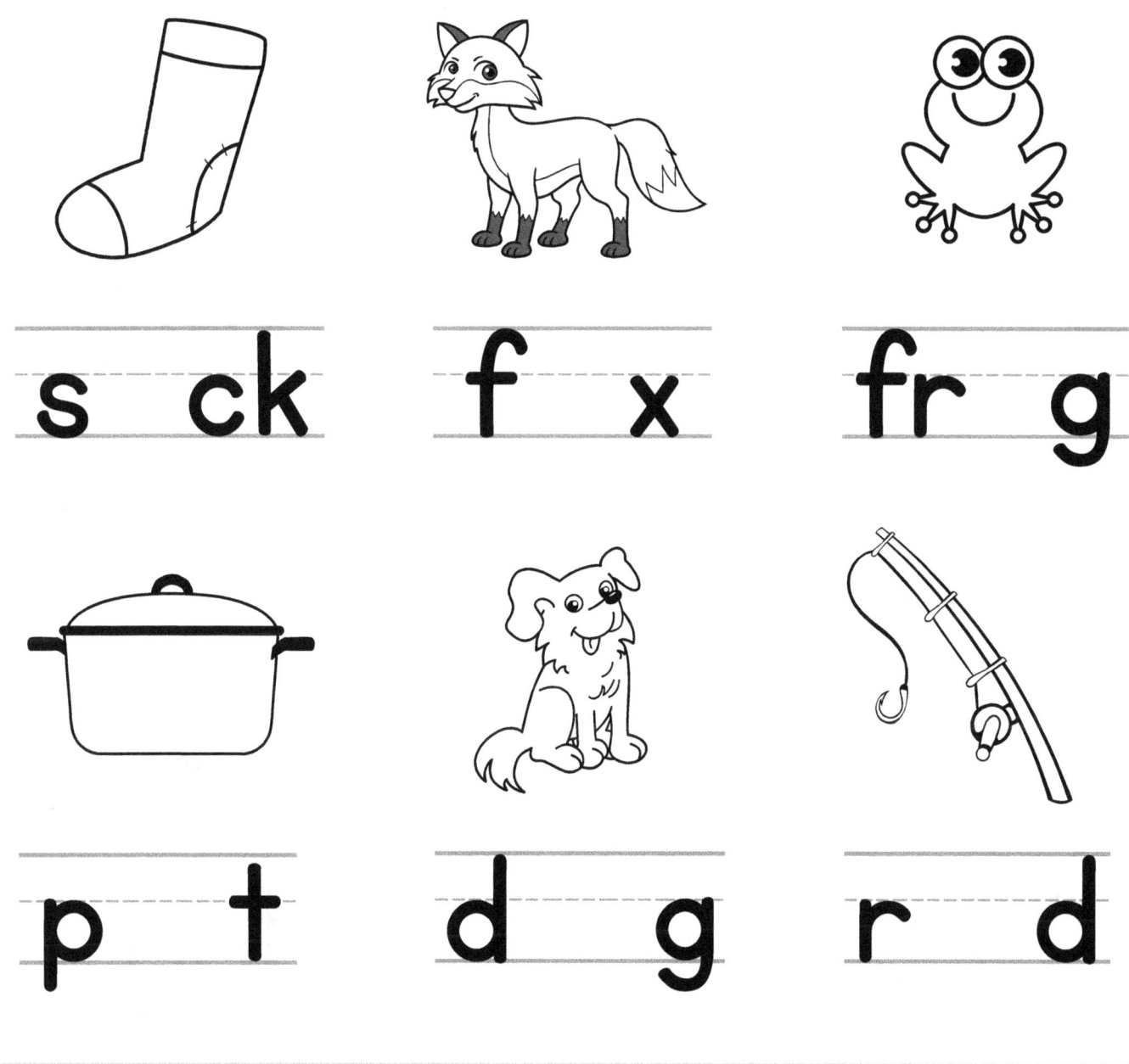

s _ ck   f _ x   fr _ g

p _ t   d _ g   r _ d

Color the sock. — black
Color the fox. — orange
Color the frog. — green
Color the pot. — red
Color the dog. — brown
Color the rod. — yellow

Short Vowel Practice: o

Say the name of the object out loud.
Draw a line from the object to the matching word.

fox

hog

frog

top

log

sock

Short Vowel Practice: o

Say the name of the object out loud.
Draw a line from the object to the matching word.

pot

rod

dog

doll

mop

box

Short Vowel Practice: o

Say the name of the object out loud.
Find the word. Look across for the word. Circle the word.

fox   frog   hog   log   sock   top

b	t	o	p	f	o	x
v	d	l	o	g	a	r
r	f	r	o	g	q	d
d	b	s	o	c	k	t
z	y	x	e	w	b	p
k	f	h	o	g	a	x

Short Vowel Practice: o

Say the name of the object out loud.
Find the word. Look across for the word. Circle the word.

box   dog   doll   mop   pot   rod

z   m   d   o   l   l   w
r   o   d   k   b   f   k
q   u   x   s   d   o   g
k   r   p   o   t   a   s
e   b   o   x   h   y   u
c   e   m   o   p   r   k

Short Vowel Practice: u

Say the name of the object out loud. Listen for the short ŭ sound. Use the color key to color the pictures.

pup

drum

bus

tub

jug

bug

Color the pup.	red	Color the tub.	blue
Color the drum.	orange	Color the jug.	green
Color the bus.	yellow	Color the bug.	purple

Short Vowel Practice: u

Say the name of the object out loud. Listen for the short ŭ sound. Use the color key to color the pictures.

sun

cup

nut

hut

plum

duck

Color the sun. 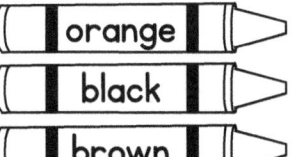 orange
Color the cup. black
Color the nut. brown

Color the hut. 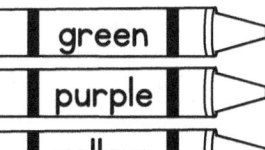 green
Color the plum. purple
Color the duck. yellow

© Chalkboard Publishing Inc.

Short Vowel Practice: u

Say the name of the object out loud. Fill in the missing vowel for each word. Use the color key to color the pictures.

t_b   j_g   b_g

p_p   dr_m   b_s

Color the tub. — red
Color the jug. — orange
Color the bug. — yellow
Color the pup. — blue
Color the drum. — green
Color the bus. — purple

Short Vowel Practice: u

Say the name of the object out loud. Fill in the missing vowel for each word. Use the color key to color the pictures.

Color the hut.	orange	Color the sun.	green
Color the plum.	black	Color the cup.	purple
Color the duck.	brown	Color the nut.	yellow

Short Vowel Practice: u

Say the name of the object out loud.
Draw a line from the object to the matching word.

jug

duck

plum

bug

hut

tub

Short Vowel Practice: u

> Say the name of the object out loud.
> Draw a line from the object to the matching word.

   bus

   sun

   drum

   cup

   pup

   nut

Short Vowel Practice: u

Say the name of the object out loud.
Find the word. Look across for the word. Circle the word.

bug   duck   hut   jug   plum   tub

t	u	b	p	l	u	m
v	j	u	g	a	t	r
r	h	e	d	u	c	k
s	c	u	e	b	u	g
p	j	n	q	g	b	p
w	h	u	t	w	c	n

Short Vowel Practice: u

Say the name of the object out loud.
Find the word. Look across for the word. Circle the word.

bus   cup   drum   nut   pup   sun

z p c u p s d
u p d r u m j
b u s l r w g
k r p b n u t
e f p u p s z
c s u n v h b

Rhyming Words

Say the name of each object out loud. Print the beginning sound to complete the word. Circle the letters that make the pair of words rhyme.

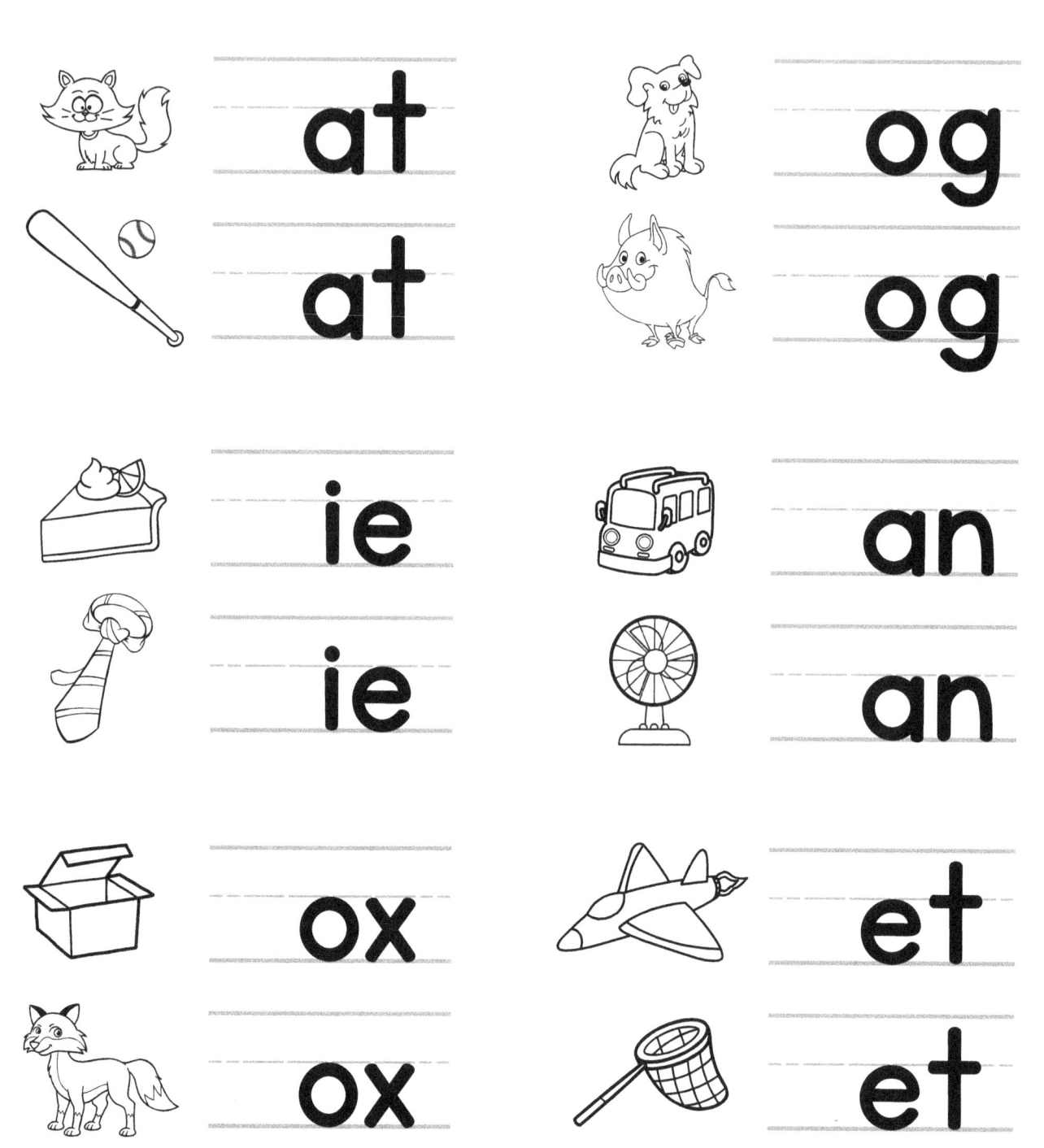

Long Vowels

Long Vowel Practice: a

Say the name of the object out loud. Listen for the long *ā* sound. Use the color key to color the pictures.

tape
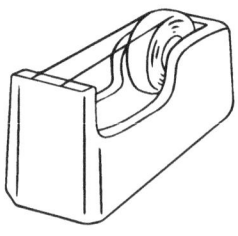

wave

ape

cane

cape

cave
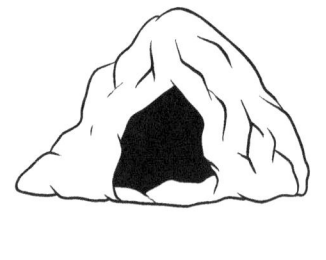

Color the tape. red
Color the wave. blue
Color the ape.   brown

Color the cane. yellow
Color the cape. blue
Color the cave. green

© Chalkboard Publishing Inc.

Long Vowel Practice: a

Say the name of the object out loud. Listen for the long *ā* sound. Use the color key to color the pictures.

cage	game	rake
	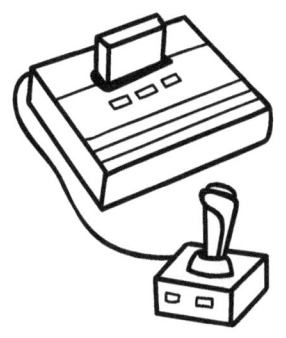	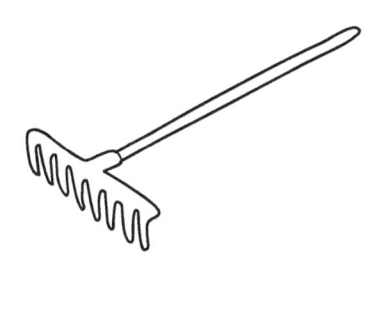
mane	plate	cake
	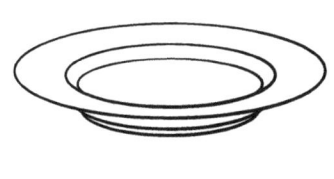	

Color the cage.   black   Color the mane.   brown
Color the game.   yellow   Color the plate. orange
Color the rake.   blue   Color the cake.   purple

© Chalkboard Publishing Inc.

69

Long Vowel Practice: a

Say the name of the object out loud. Fill in the missing vowel.
Use the color key to color the pictures.

t_pe   w_ve   _pe

c_ne   c_pe   c_ve

Color the tape. red
Color the wave. blue
Color the ape.   brown
Color the cane. yellow
Color the cape. purple
Color the cave. green

Long Vowel Practice: a

Say the name of the object out loud. Fill in the missing vowel. Use the color key to color the pictures.

c___ge

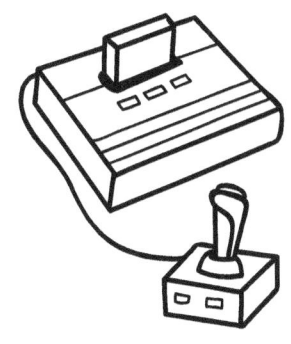
g___me

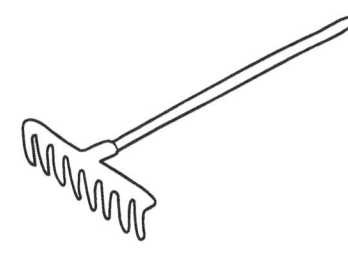
r___ke

m___ne

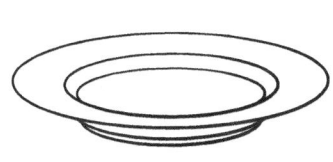
pl___te

c___ke

Color the cage. pink
Color the game. yellow
Color the rake. blue
Color the mane. brown
Color the plate. orange
Color the cake. purple

Long Vowel Practice: a

Say the name of the object out loud.
Draw a line from the object to the matching word.

game

tape

rake

cape

cage

ape

Long Vowel Practice: a

Say the name of the object out loud.
Draw a line from the object to the matching word.

   wave

   plate

   mane

   cake

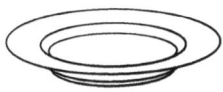   cave

   cane

Long Vowel Practice: a

Read the words in the word box out loud. Read the sentence. Fill in the blank with a word from the word box.

ape   cape   cave   plate   tape

I put _____ on the box.

I saw an _____ at the zoo.

The _____ is long.

The _____ is clean.

The _____ is dark.

Long Vowel Practice: a

Read the word out loud. Print the word. Circle the object that matches the word.

tape

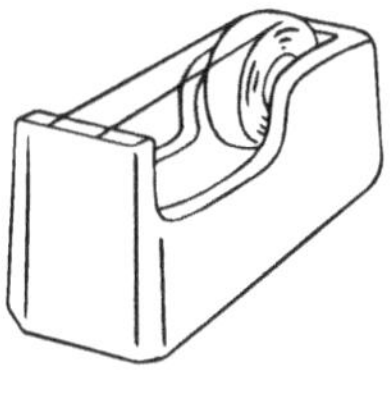

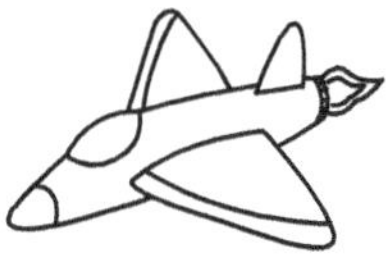

cape

ape

cage

game

rake

Long Vowel Practice: e

Say the name of the object out loud. Listen for the long ē sound. Use the color key to color the pictures.

bee

tree

seal

jeep

feet

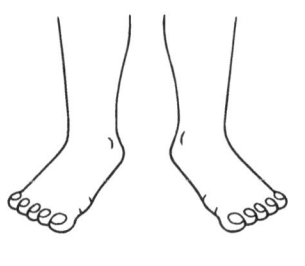

seed

Color the bee. 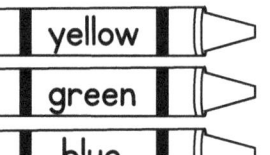 yellow
Color the tree. green
Color the seal. blue

Color the jeep. 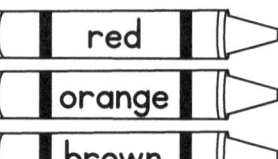 red
Color the feet. orange
Color the seed. brown

Long Vowel Practice: e

Say the name of the object out loud. Listen for the long ē sound. Use the color key to color the pictures.

sheep

deer

ear
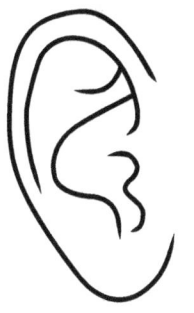

meal

leaf

beak

Color the sheep.	black	Color the meal.	red
Color the deer.	green	Color the leaf.	brown
Color the ear.	blue	Color the beak.	yellow

© Chalkboard Publishing Inc.

Long Vowel Practice: e

Say the name of the object out loud. Fill in the missing vowel for each word. Use the color key to color the pictures.

  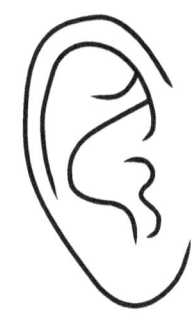

sh __ ep   d __ er   __ ar

m __ al   l __ af   b __ ak

Color the sheep.	black	Color the meal.	red
Color the deer.	green	Color the leaf.	brown
Color the ear.	blue	Color the beak.	yellow

Long Vowel Practice: e

Say the name of the object out loud.
Draw a line from the object to the matching word.

tree

sheep

deer

ear

bee

seal

Long Vowel Practice: e

Say the name of the object out loud.
Draw a line from the object to the matching word.

feet

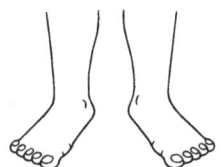

jeep

meal

leaf

beak

seed

© Chalkboard Publishing Inc.

Long Vowel Practice: e

Read the words in the word box out loud. Read the sentence. Fill in the blank with a word from the word box.

bee   feet   jeep   seal   tree

The _____ makes honey.

I saw a _____ at the zoo.

I have two _____ .

The _____ is fast.

The _____ is tall.

82

Long Vowel Practice: e

Read the word out loud. Print the word. Circle the object that matches the word.

Long Vowel Practice: i

Say the name of the object out loud. Circle long vowel i. Use the color key to color the pictures.

ice
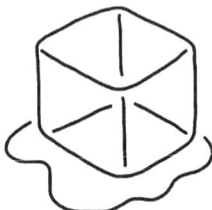

dice

tire

nine

fire

five

Color the ice.   blue
Color the dice. red
Color the tire. black

Color the nine. green
Color the fire. orange
Color the five. purple

Long Vowel Practice: i

Say the name of the object out loud. Circle long vowel i. Use the color key to color the pictures.

slide

vine

bride

pie

dime

hive

Color the slide. 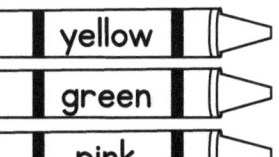 yellow   Color the pie. 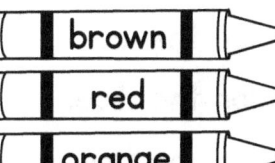 brown
Color the vine. green   Color the dime. red
Color the bride. pink   Color the hive. orange

Long Vowel Practice: i

Say the name of the object out loud. Fill in the missing vowel for each word. Use the color key to color the pictures.

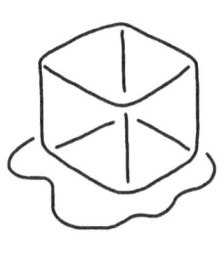  

__ce   d__ce   t__re

  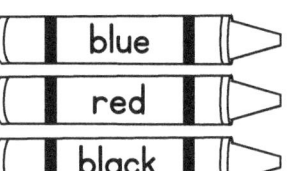

n__ne   f__re   f__ve

Color the ice. | blue | Color the nine. | green |
Color the dice. | red | Color the fire. | orange |
Color the tire. | black| Color the five. | purple |

Long Vowel Practice: i

Say the name of the object out loud. Fill in the missing vowel for each word. Use the color key to color the pictures.

sl_de   v_ne   br_de

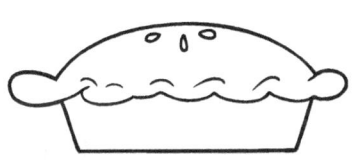  

p_e   d_me   h_ve

Color the slide. 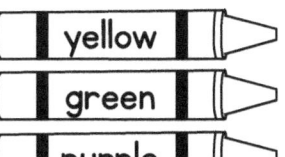 yellow   Color the pie. 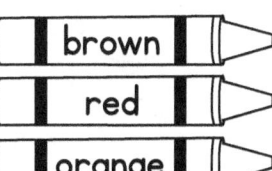 brown
Color the vine.   green   Color the dime. red
Color the bride. purple   Color the hive. orange

Long Vowel Practice: i

Say the name of the object out loud.
Draw a line from the object to the matching word.

   dice

   tire

   vine

   bride

   slide

   ice

Long Vowel Practice: i

Say the name of the object out loud.
Draw a line from the object to the matching word.

   dime

   hive

   nine

   fire

   five

   pie

Long Vowel Practice: i

Read the words in the word box out loud. Read the sentence. Fill in the blank with a word from the word box.

| dime | fire | ice | pie | slide |

I have a _____.

I like _____.

The _____ is fun.

The _____ is cold.

The _____ is hot.

Long Vowel Practice: i

Read the word out loud. Print the word. Circle the object that matches the word.

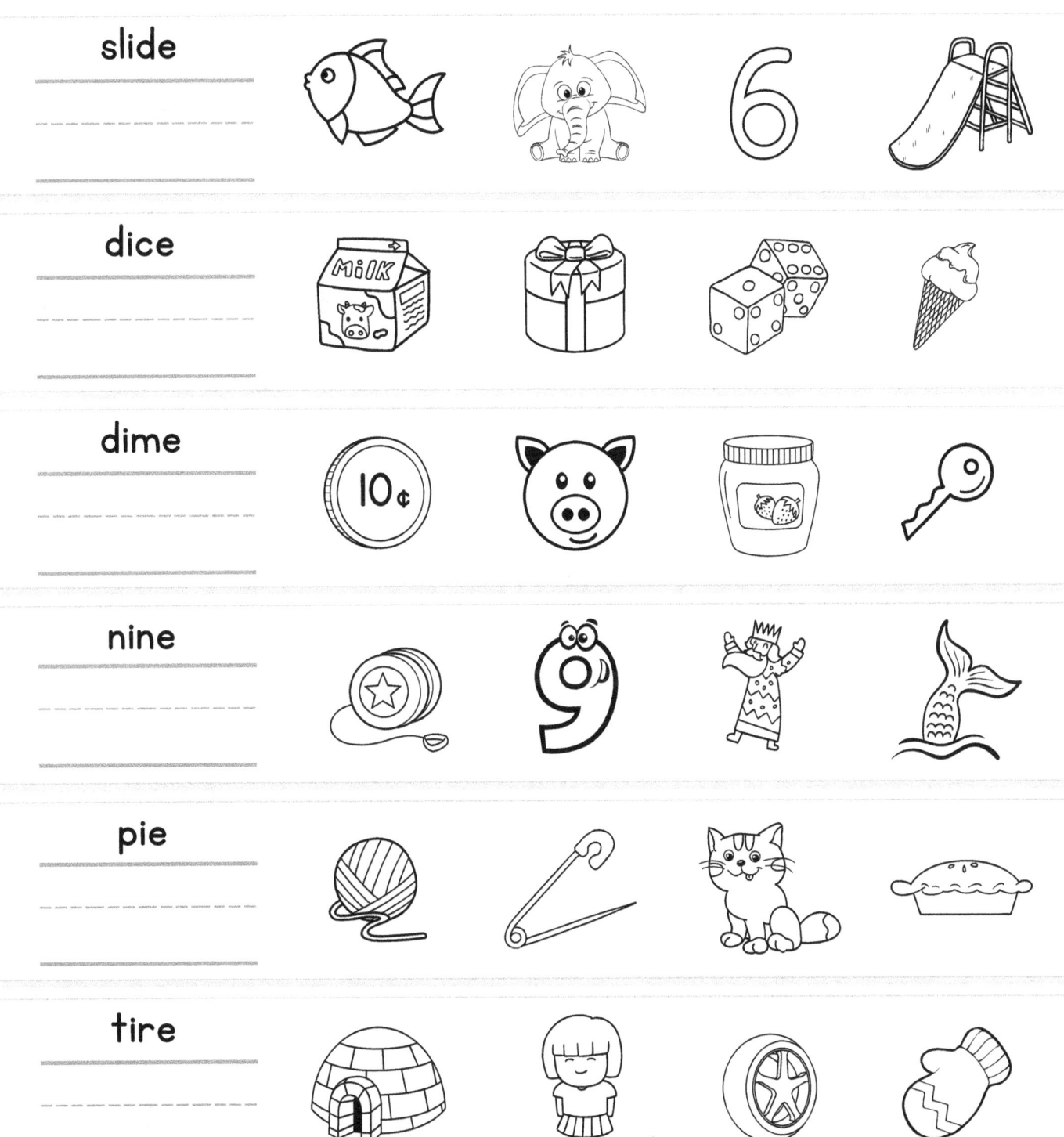

Long Vowel Practice: o

Say the name of the object out loud. Listen for the long ō sound. Use the color key to color the pictures.

robe

rope
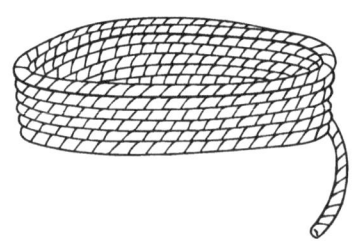

phone

cone

pole

rose

Color the robe. blue
Color the rope. yellow
Color the phone. black

Color the cone. green
Color the pole. purple
Color the rose. red

Long Vowel Practice: o

Say the name of the object out loud. Listen for the long ō sound. Use the color key to color the pictures.

note

globe

nose
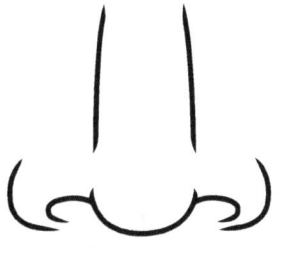

hose

bone

stove

Color the note.	black	Color the hose.	brown
Color the globe.	blue	Color the bone.	orange
Color the nose.	red	Color the stove.	purple

Long Vowel Practice: o

Say the name of the object out loud. Fill in the missing vowel for each word. Use the color key to color the pictures.

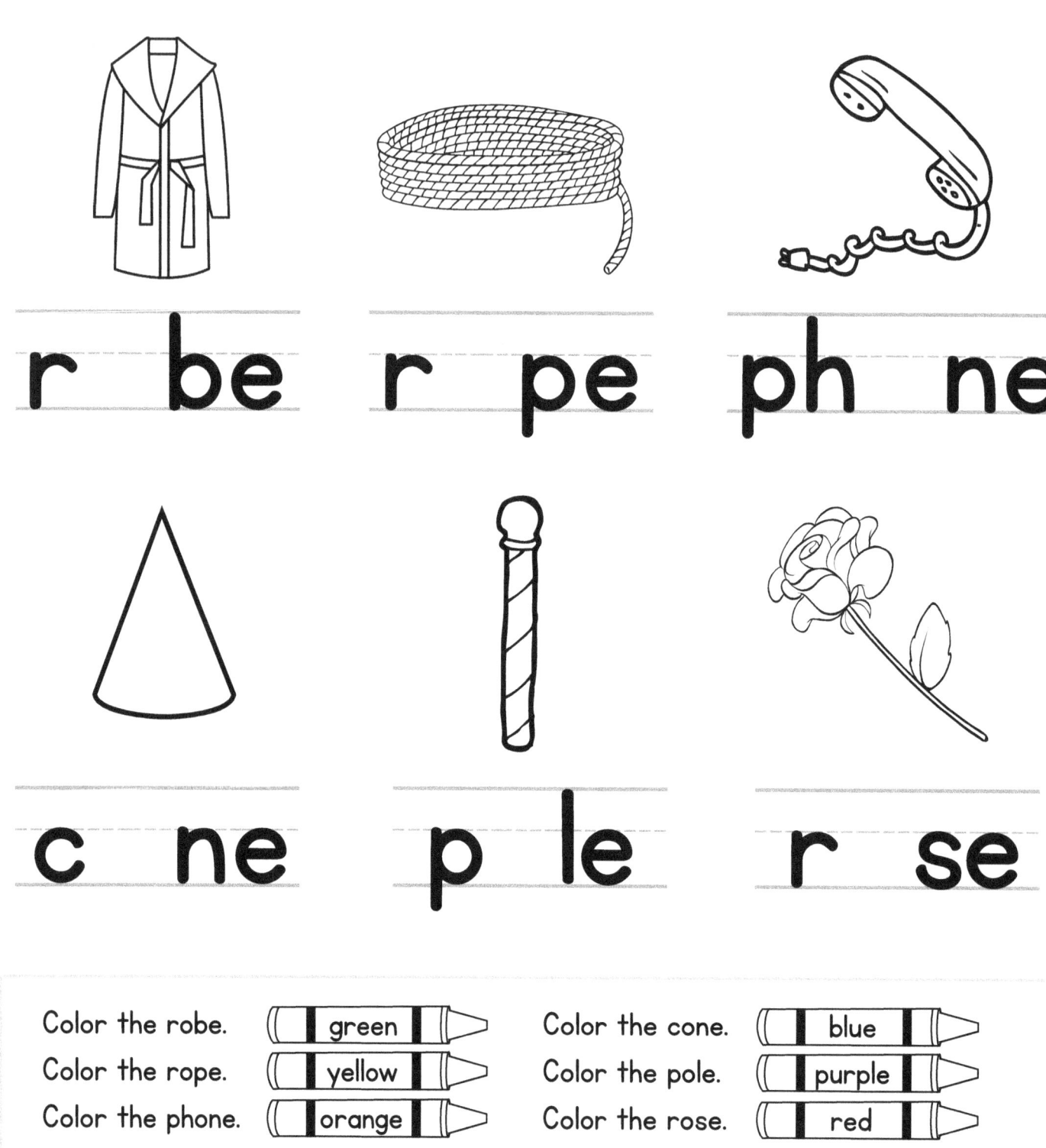

r__be   r__pe   ph__ne

c__ne   p__le   r__se

Color the robe. green
Color the rope. yellow
Color the phone. orange
Color the cone. blue
Color the pole. purple
Color the rose. red

Long Vowel Practice: o

Say the name of the object out loud. Fill in the missing vowel for each word. Use the color key to color the pictures.

n__te    gl__be 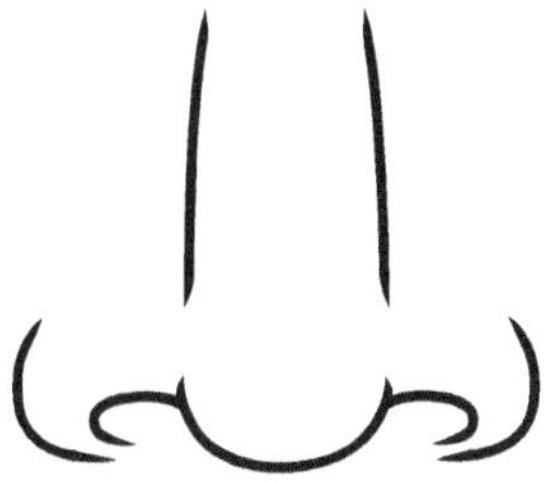   n__se

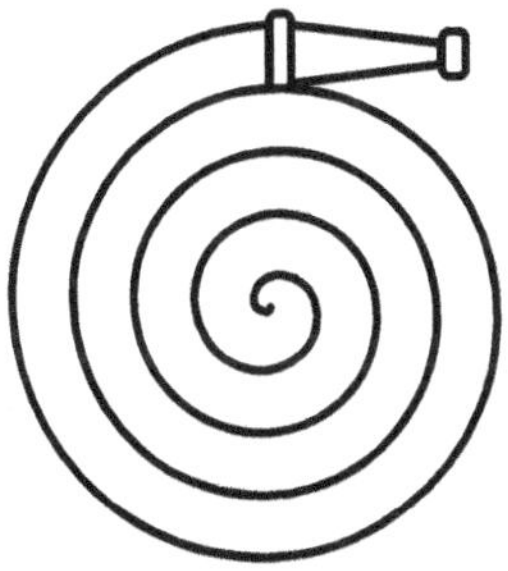

h__se    b__ne    st__ve

Color the note. — black
Color the globe. — blue
Color the nose. — red
Color the hose. — brown
Color the bone. — orange
Color the stove. — purple

Long Vowel Practice: o

Say the name of the object out loud.
Draw a line from the object to the matching word.

   phone

   robe

   rope

   globe

   nose

cone

Long Vowel Practice: o

Say the name of the object out loud.
Draw a line from the object to the matching word.

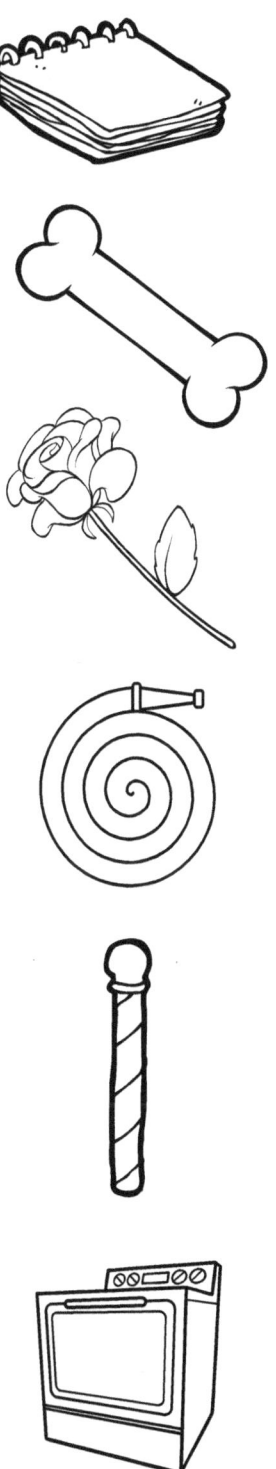

stove

hose

bone

note

rose

pole

Long Vowel Practice: o

Read the words in the word box out loud. Read the sentence. Fill in the blank with a word from the word box.

| nose | phone | robe | rope | rose |

I smell with my _____.

My _____ is cozy.

I talk on the _____.

The _____ is pretty.

The _____ is long.

Long Vowel Practice: o

Read the word out loud. Print the word. Circle the object that matches the word.

Long Vowel Practice: u

Say the name of the object out loud. Listen for the long $\bar{u}$ sound. Use the color key to color the pictures.

cube
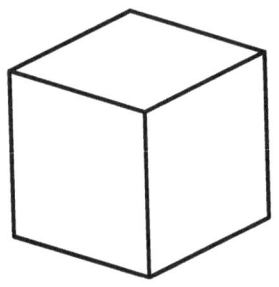

argue

June

mule

menu

fuel
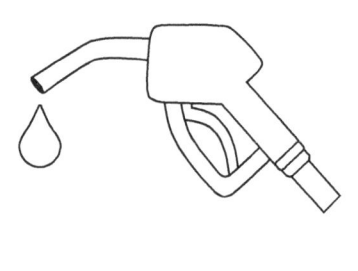

Color the cube. — purple
Color argue. — black
Color June. — yellow

Color the mule. — brown
Color the menu. — yellow
Color the fuel. — green

Long Vowel Practice: u

Say the name of the object out loud. Listen for the long ū sound. Use the color key to color the pictures.

huge 	unit 	unicycle 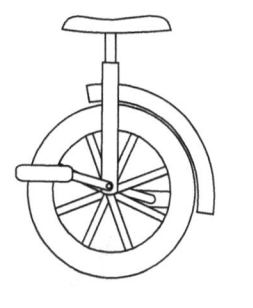
cute 	unicorn 	rescue 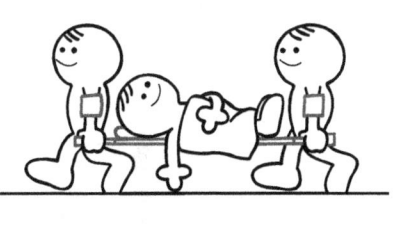

Color the huge T-rex. — red
Color the unit. — yellow
Color the unicycle. — orange
Color the cute cat. — blue
Color the unicorn. — green
Color the rescue. — brown

Long Vowel Practice: u

Say the name of the object out loud. Fill in the missing vowel for each word. Use the color key to color the pictures.

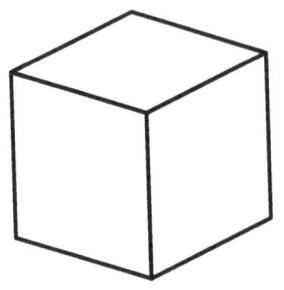  

c_be   arg_e   J_ne

  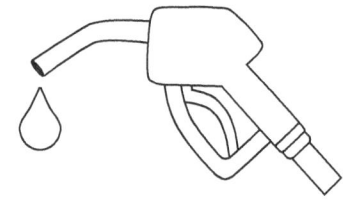

m_le   men_   f_el

Color the cube. — purple   Color the mule. — brown
Color argue. — black   Color the menu. — yellow
Color June. — yellow   Color the fuel. — green

Long Vowel Practice: u

Say the name of the object out loud. Fill in the missing vowel for each word. Use the color key to color the pictures.

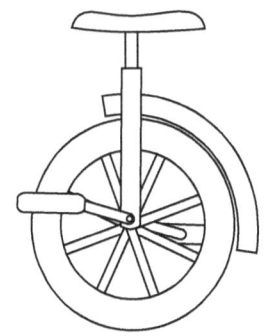

h_ge   _nit   _nicycle

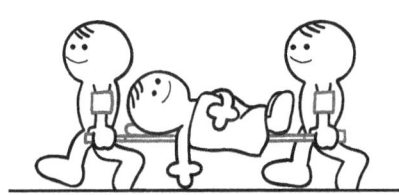

c_te   _nicorn   resc_e

Color the huge T-rex. red   Color the cute cat. blue
Color the unit.   yellow   Color the unicorn.   green
Color the unicycle.   orange   Color the rescue.   brown

Long Vowel Practice: u

Say the name of the object out loud.
Draw a line from the object to the matching word.

huge

fuel

argue

unicycle

cube

June

Long Vowel Practice: u

Say the name of the object out loud.
Draw a line from the object to the matching word.

rescue

unicorn

cute

menu

unit

mule

Long Vowel Practice: u

Read the words in the word box out loud. Read the sentence. Fill in the blank with a word from the word box.

| cute | huge | June | menu | unicorn |

I like the _____ cat.

_____ is warm.

I want to find a _____ .

I read the _____ .

The dinosaur is _____ .

Long Vowel Practice: u

Read the word out loud. Print the word.
Circle the object that matches the word.

June

argue

mule

huge

rescue

cube

© Chalkboard Publishing Inc.

107

Y as Long i Sound

Sometimes the letter y makes a long *i* sound.

fly	sky	cry	fry
			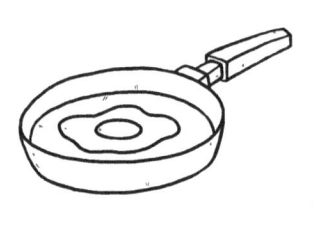

Y as Long e Sound

Sometimes the letter y makes a long *e* sound.

bunny	baby	lady	puppy

Y as Long Vowel Sounds: Review

Each word below has one of the two y sounds. Circle the correct answer for each word.

Long ē
Long ī

Long ē
Long ī

Long ē
Long ī

Long ē
Long ī

Long ē
Long ī

Long ē
Long ī

Long ē
Long ī

Long ē
Long ī

Long ē
Long ī

Long and Short Vowel Review

Say the name of the object out loud.
Draw a line from the object to the matching word.

cape   cap

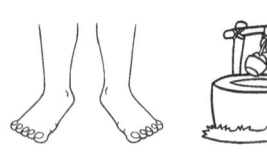

well   feet

pin   pie

June   jug

ant   ape

hog   stove

cane   can

cup   cube

net   tree

Circle all the words with a long vowel. 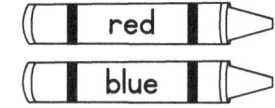 red
Circle all the words with a short vowel. blue

Long and Short Vowel Review

Say the name of the object out loud.
Draw a line from the object to the matching word.

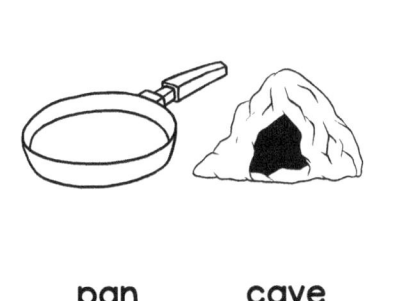

pan   cave

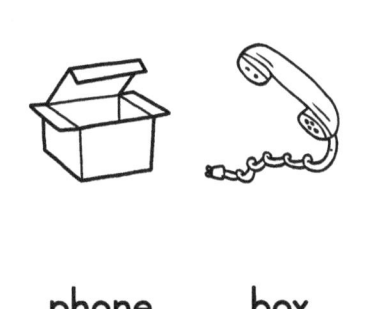

phone   box

egg   deer

cute   cube

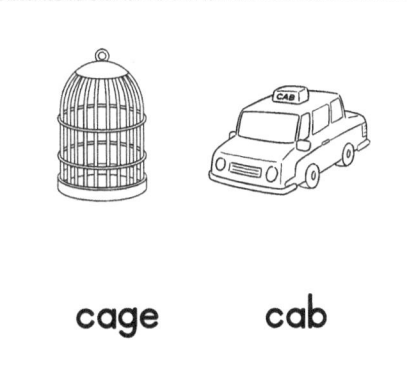

cage   cab

bed   tree

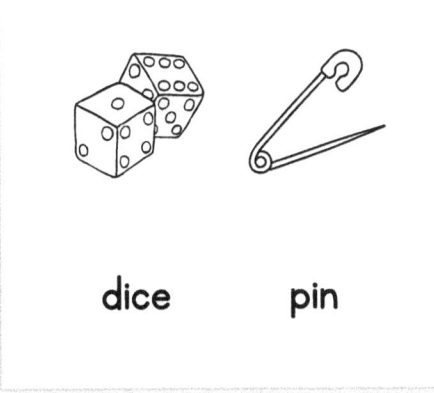

dice   pin

milk   dime

sock   rope

Circle all the words with a long vowel. 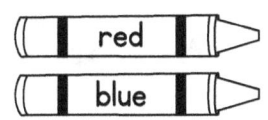 red
Circle all the words with a short vowel. blue

Rhyming Words

Say the name of the object out loud. Print the beginning sound to complete the word. Circle the letters that make the pair of words rhyme.

Beginning Letter Sounds

Beginning Letters Sounds: Match Up

Say the letter at the beginning of the row out loud. Circle the objects that begin with that letter sound.

o	owl	zipper	octopus
g	goat	guitar	spoon
q	cat	quill	quilt
t	train	tree	moon
b	ball	book	duck

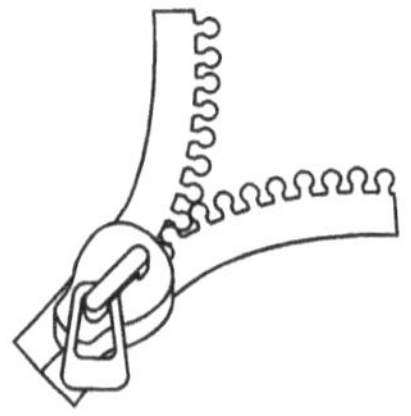

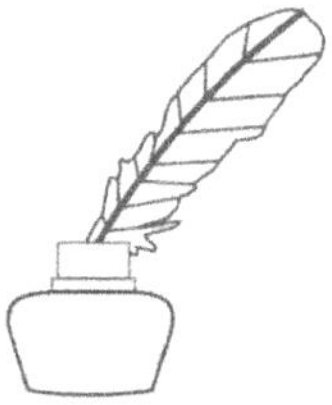

Beginning Letters Sounds: Match Up

Say the letter at the beginning of the row out loud. Circle the objects that begin with that letter sound.

Identifying Beginning Sounds

Say the name of the object out loud.
Color in the beginning sound for the object's name.

Identifying Beginning Sounds

Say the name of the object out loud.
Color in the beginning sound for the object's name.

Identifying Beginning Sounds

Say the name of the object out loud. Print the letter that shows the beginning sound for the object's name. Choose from the letters on the right.

Beginning Sounds

Say the name of the object out loud. Print the letter that is the beginning sound for the object's name.

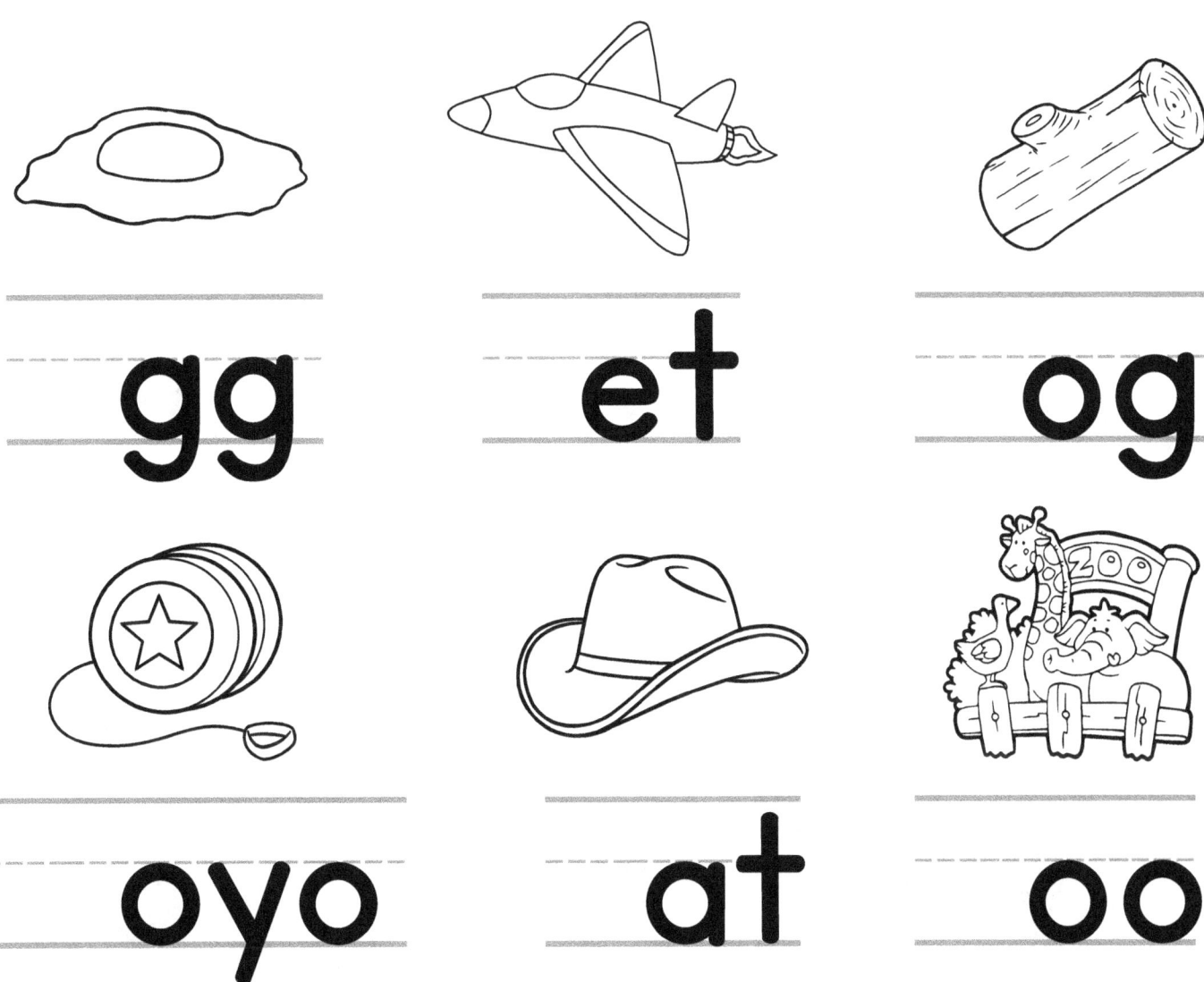

Color the egg.	black	Color the yoyo.	brown
Color the jet.	yellow	Color the hat.	orange
Color the log.	blue	Color the zoo.	green

Beginning Sounds

Say the name of the object out loud. Print the letter that is the beginning sound for the object's name.

___uill

___et

___ey

___wl

___est

___ap

Color the quil.   red
Color the net.   purple
Color the key.   blue
Color the owl.   orange
Color the vest.   yellow
Color the cap.   green

Beginning Letter Sounds: Match Up

Say the name of the object out loud. Draw a line to connect the objects that have the same beginning sounds.

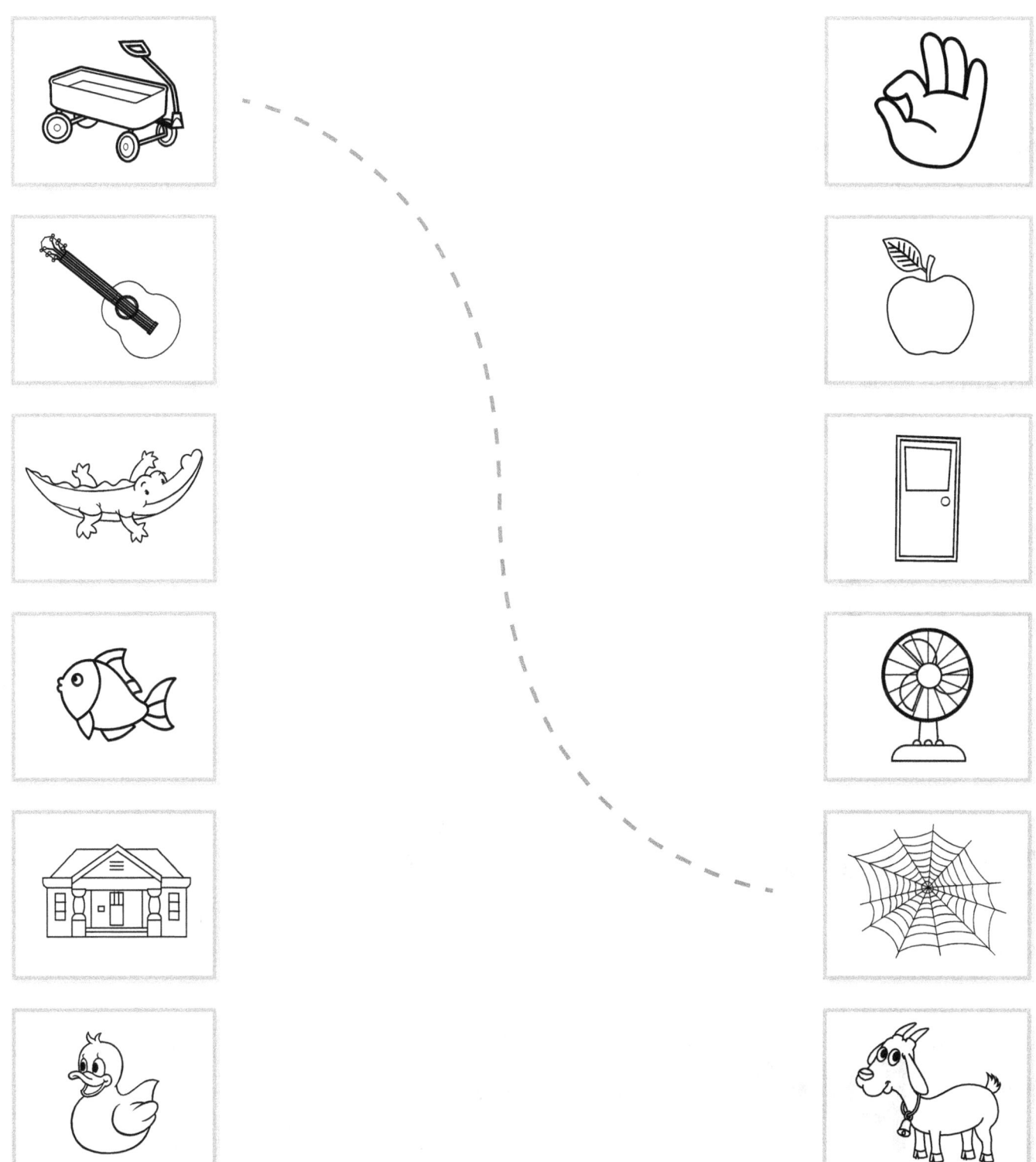

Beginning Sounds: Rhyming Fun

Change the letter that makes the beginning sound. Print the new rhyming word on the line.

Change  to  _____

Change  to  _____

Change  to  _____

Change  to  _____

Change  to  _____

Beginning Sounds: Rhyming Fun

Change the letter that makes the beginning sound. Print the new rhyming word on the line.

Change **dog** to  _____

Change **mug** to  _____

Change **red** to 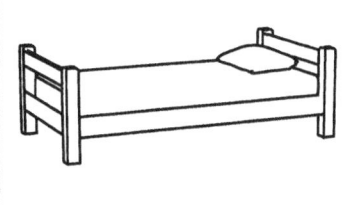 _____

Change **man** to  _____

Change **fin** to 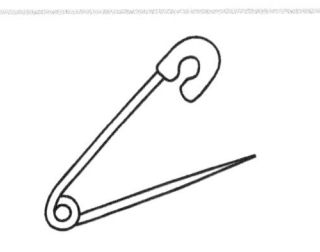 _____

Ending Letter Sounds

Ending Letter Sounds

Say the name of the object out loud. Color in the ending sound for the object's name.

Ending Letter Sounds

Say the name of the object out loud. Color in the ending sound for the object's name.

Ending Letter Sounds

Circle the objects that have the same ending sound as the word.

cat

jam

dog

mop

pen

Ending Letter Sounds

Circle the objects that have the same ending sound as the word.

sled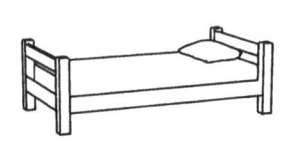

ball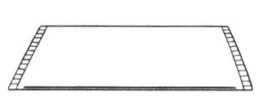

bus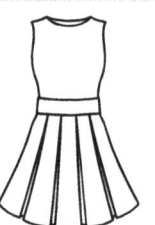

ox

sip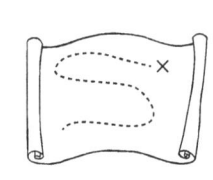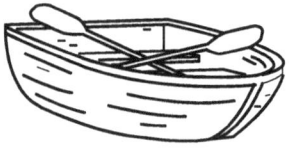

Identifying Ending Sounds

Say the name of the object out loud. Print the letter that shows the ending sound for the object's name. Choose from the letters on the right.

Identifying Ending Sounds

Say the name of the object out loud.
Circle the ending sound for the object's name.

Ending Sounds

Say the name of the object out loud. Print the letter that is the ending sound for the object's name.

boo   ba   han

bu   tu   ca

Color the book.	black	Color the bug.	red
Color the bat.	yellow	Color the tub.	orange
Color the hand.	blue	Color the car.	green

© Chalkboard Publishing Inc.

131

Ending Sounds

Say the name of the object out loud. Print the letter that is the ending sound for the object's name.

sta   ho   pai

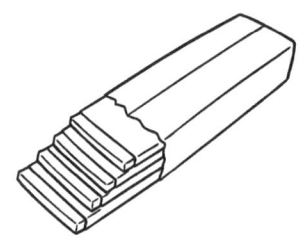  

gu   fa   he

Color the star.	yellow	Color the gum.	black
Color the hog.	brown	Color the fan.	orange
Color the pail.	red	Color the hen.	blue

Beginning and Ending Sounds

Beginning and Ending Sounds Review

Say the name of the object out loud. Complete the word by printing the beginning and ending letter sounds. Color the pictures.

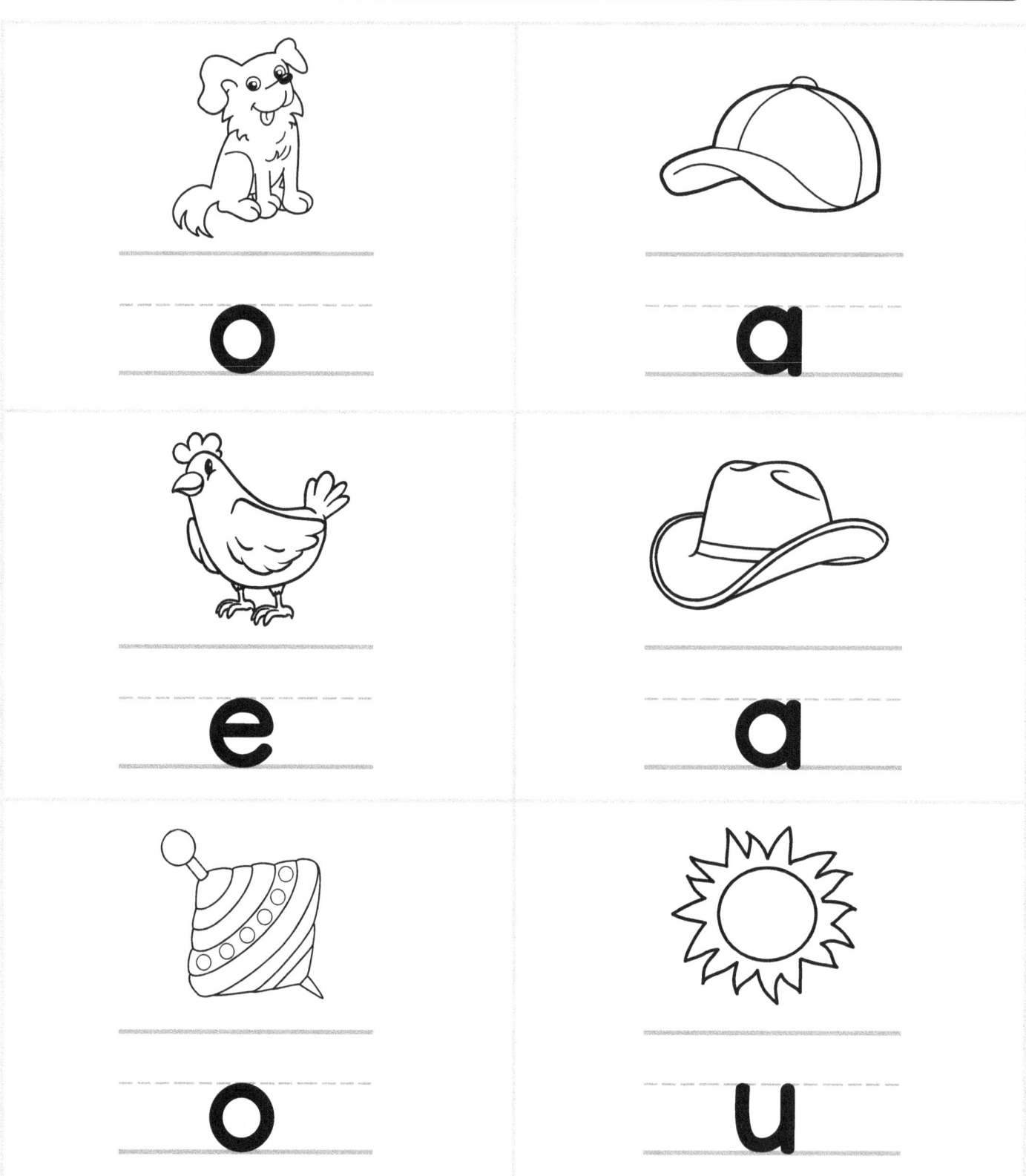

Beginning and Ending Sounds Review

Say the name of the object out loud. Complete the word by printing the beginning and ending letter sounds. Color the pictures.

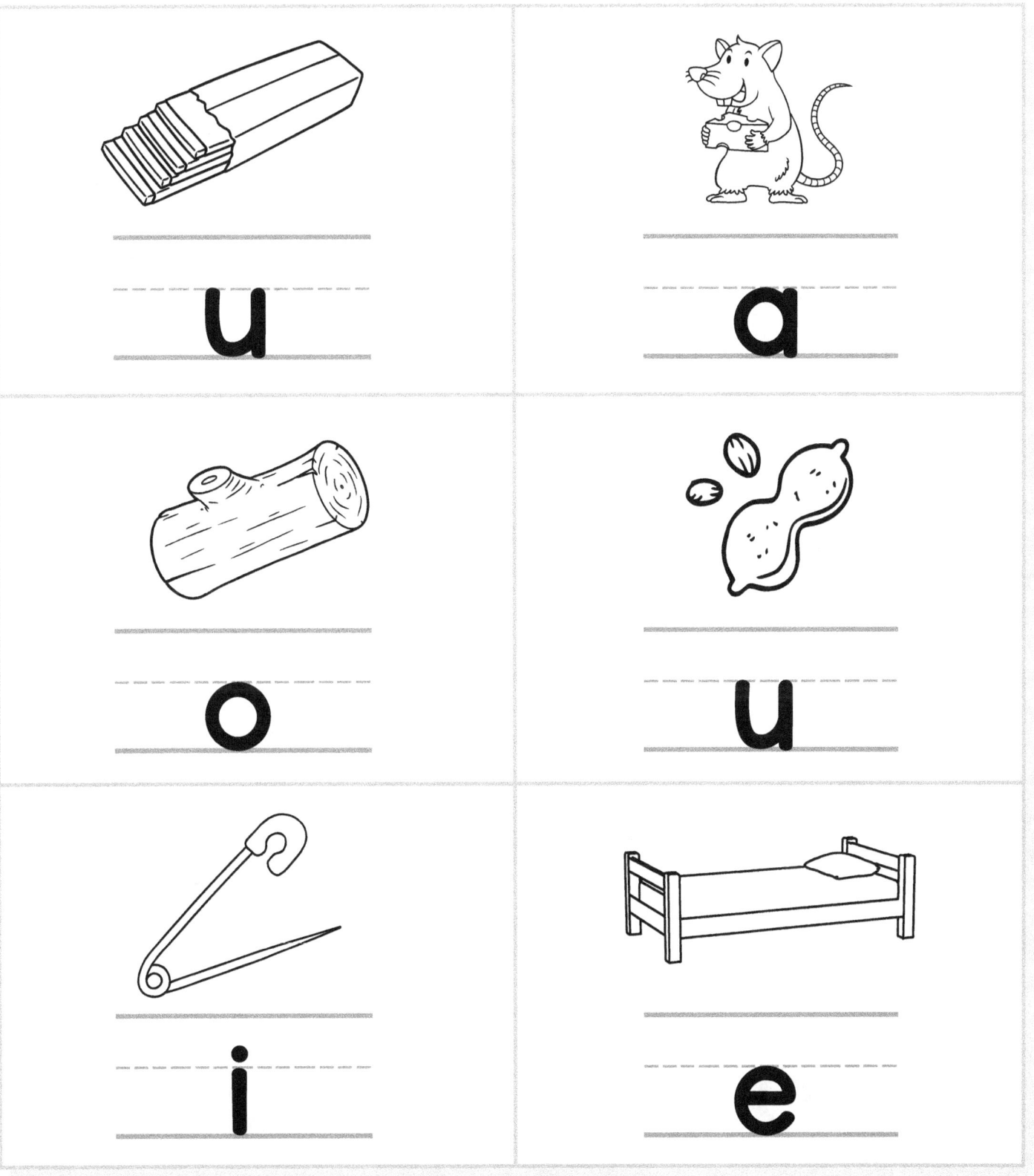

Beginning and Ending Sounds Review

Say the name of the object out loud. Complete the word by printing the beginning and ending letter sounds. Color the pictures.

Beginning and Ending Sounds Review

Say the name of the object out loud. Complete the word by printing the beginning and ending letter sounds. Color the pictures.

Consonant Blends

s blends

skunk

sloth

smile

spill

scarf

snack

star

sweet

r blends

brush

grapes

crab

dragon

frame

print

truck

l blends

black

clam

glove

fly

plum

Consonant Blends with s

Say the name of the object out loud. Circle the correct consonant blend or beginning sounds for the object's name.

sl sp	sk sc	sn sw
		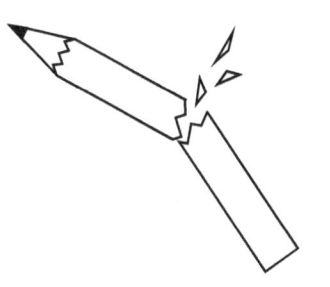

sw sm	sl st	st sk

sw sm	sp sl	sn sk
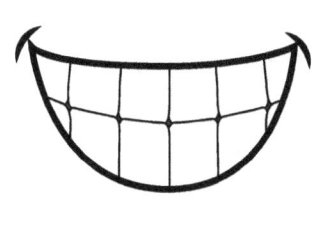		

Consonant Blends with s

Say the name of the object out loud. Circle the correct consonant blend or beginning sounds for the object's name.

sc   sp

sk   sp

sn   st

st   sl

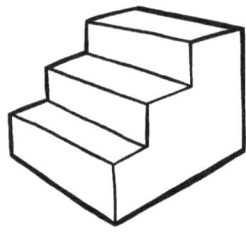

sk   sp

sk   sm

sl   sp

sk   sn

sm   sp

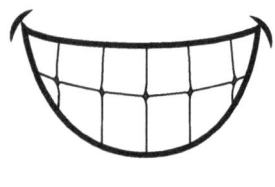

Consonant Blends with s

Say the name of the object out loud.
Fill in the missing consonant blend or beginning sounds for the word.

sc sp	sk sp	sl sn
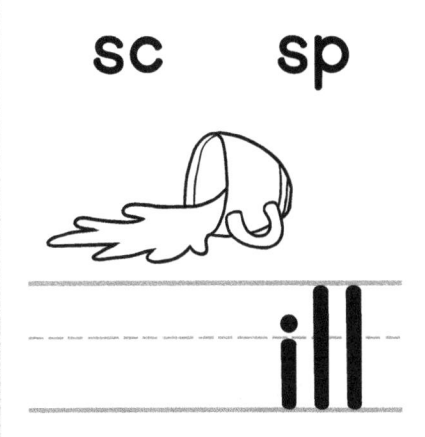 ill	 ate	 ip

sl sw	sk sn	sp sl
 ide	 unk	 ed

sm sc	sp sm	sc sm
 ell	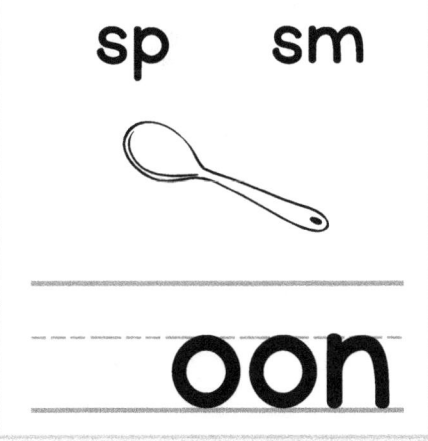 oon	 ile

Consonant Blends with s

Say the name of the object out loud.
Fill in the missing consonant blend or beginning sounds for the word.

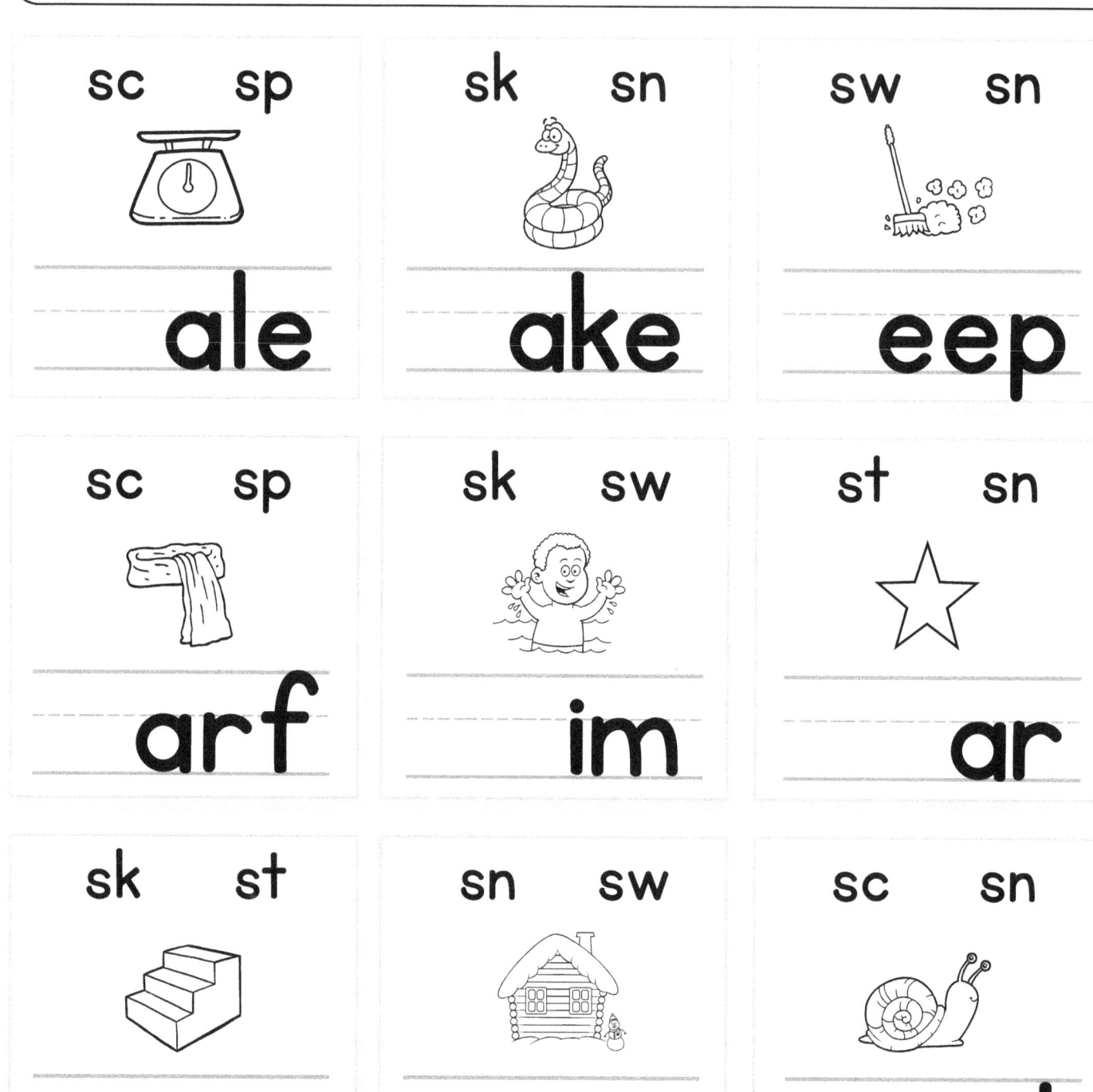

Consonant Blends with s

Say the name of the object out loud. Color the object with the same beginning sound as the first object in the row.

sk				
sl				
sm				
sp				
sc				
sn				

Consonant Blends with s

Say the name of the object out loud. Color the object with the same beginning sound as the first object in the row.

st				
sw				
sk				
sm				
sc				
sl				

Consonant Blends with s

Read the sentence.
Fill in the blank with a consonant blend from the word box.

| sc | sl | sm | sn | st | sw |

The _____ide is fun.

The _____ail is slow.

I like to _____im.

I wear a _____arf.

I wish upon a _____ar.

I can _____ell the flower.

Consonant Blends with r

Say the name of the object out loud. Circle the correct consonant blend or beginning sounds for the object's name.

br fr	pr gr	dr cr

dr pr	dr cr	br tr

fr pr	cr fr	tr br

Consonant Blends with r

Say the name of the object out loud. Circle the correct consonant blend or beginning sounds for the object's name.

br cr	pr tr	br fr
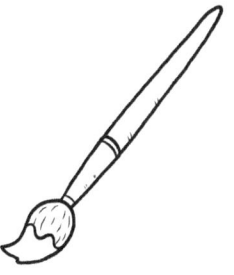		

gr tr	cr dr	fr pr

br dr	cr fr	dr tr

Consonant Blends with r

Say the name of the object out loud. Fill in the missing consonant blend or beginning sounds for the object's name.

br   cr   dr   fr   gr   pr   tr

__int

__ab

__ink

__ead

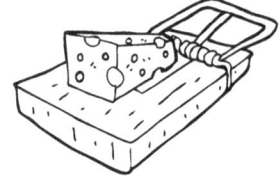
__ap

__as

__ize

__uit

__oom

Consonant Blends with r

Say the name of the object out loud. Fill in the missing consonant blend or beginning sounds for the object's name.

br   cr   dr   fr   gr   pr   tr

___ y

___ ide

___ oom

___ ick

___ ack

___ ip

___ uck

___ ib

___ ess

Consonant Blends with r

Say the name of the object out loud. Color the picture with the same beginning sound as the first object in the row.

br				
cr				
dr				
fr				
gr				
pr				
tr				

Consonant Blends with r

Read the sentence.
Fill in the blank with a consonant blend from the word box.

| br | cr | dr | fr | gr | pr |

The _____ead is fresh.

The _____ane is big.

I like my _____iend.

The _____agon is cute.

I _____ess the button.

The _____apes are tasty.

Consonant Blends with r

Say the name of the object out loud.
Find the word. Look across for the word. Circle the word.

brick   crab   drip   grass   prize   train

c r a b p w e
v s d r i p k
r x p r i z e
t r a i n g j
s b r i c k a
g r a s s q u

Consonant Blends with l

Say the name of the object out loud. Circle the correct consonant blend or beginning sounds for the object's name.

bl pl	gl fl	bl cl
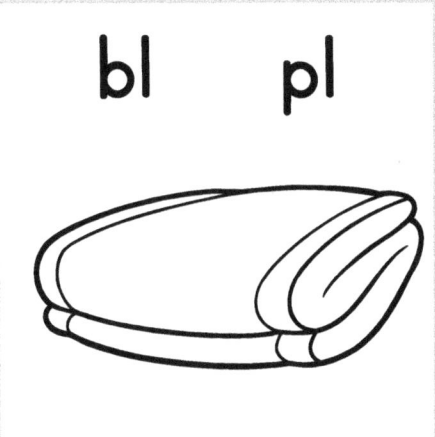		
pl cl	gl bl	fl cl
	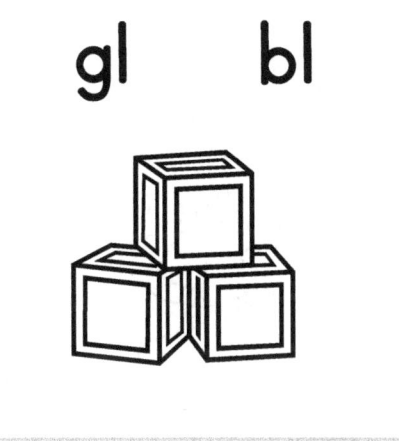	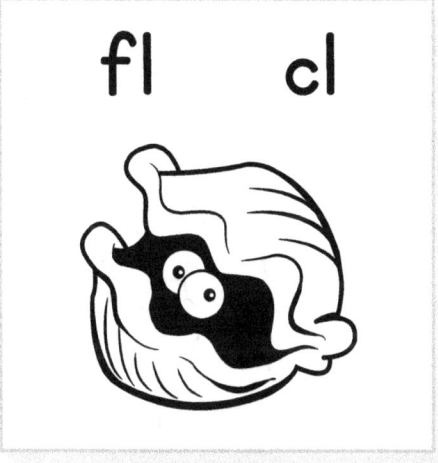
gl bl	bl pl	cl fl

© Chalkboard Publishing Inc.

Consonant Blends with l

Say the name of the object out loud. Circle the correct consonant blend or beginning sounds for the object's name.

pl cl	fl bl	pl bl
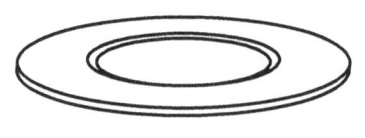		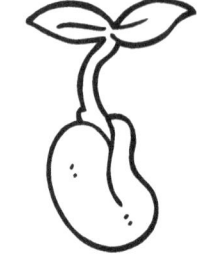

bl fl	pl gl	cl pl
		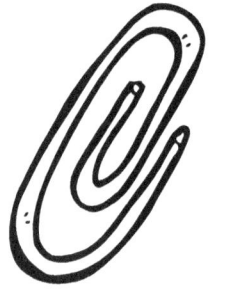

fl cl	gl cl	gl bl
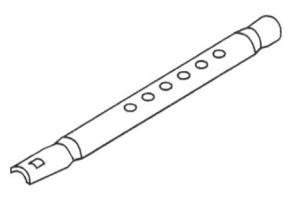		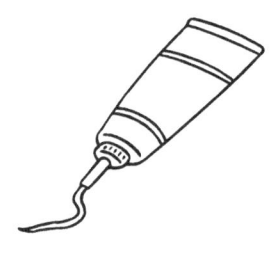

Consonant Blends with l

Say the name of the object out loud. Fill in the missing consonant blend or beginning sounds for the object's name.

bl   cl   fl   gl   pl

__ack

__ock

__ove

__am

__ug

__y

__ame

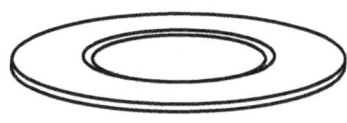
__ate

__over

© Chalkboard Publishing Inc.

Consonant Blends with l

Say the name of the object out loud. Fill in the missing consonant blend or beginning sounds for the object's name.

bl**cl****fl****gl****pl**

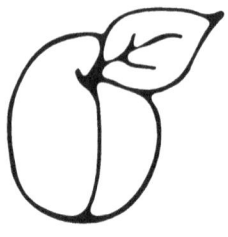
__ um

__ ue

__ own

__ ug

__ oud

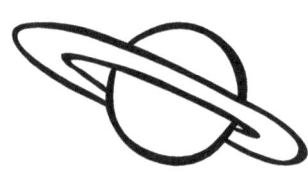
__ anet

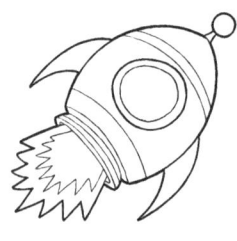
__ ast

__ itter

__ oss

Consonant Blends with l

Say the name of the object out loud. Color the picture with the same beginning sound as the first object in the row.

bl

cl

fl

gl

pl

Consonant Blends with l

Read the sentence.
Fill in the blank with a consonant blend from the word box.

| bl | cl | fl | gl | pl |

The ___anket is soft.

The ___over is lucky.

I like to play the ___ute.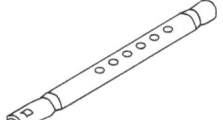

The ___ue is sticky.

The ___anet is in space.

The ___itter is pretty.

Consonant Blends with l

Say the name of the object out loud.
Find the word. Look across for the word. Circle the word.

block   clam   flag   glass   plug

b	b	o	c	k	w	e
v	d	c	l	a	m	d
r	s	f	l	a	g	e
p	l	u	g	h	f	m
d	f	i	p	w	b	p
t	g	l	a	s	s	f

Congratulations!
Great Work!

_____ can identify:

- **Beginning Letter Sounds**
- **Ending Letter Sounds**
- **Consonant Blends**
- **Short Vowels**
- **Long Vowels**

www.ingramcontent.com/pod-product-compliance
Lightning Source LLC
Chambersburg PA
CBHW080603090426
42735CB00016B/3328